...AN
...S

Compiled and Edited by

Carol L. Newbill

Oxmoor
House®

©1997 by Oxmoor House, Inc.

Book Division of Southern Progress Corporation

P.O. Box 2463, Birmingham, AL 35201

Published by Oxmoor House, Inc., and Leisure Arts, Inc.

Library of Congress Catalog Card Number: 86-62283

ISBN: 0-8487-1617-5

ISSN: 1076-7673

Manufactured in the United States of America

First Printing 1997

Editor-in-Chief: Nancy Fitzpatrick Wyatt

Senior Crafts Editor: Susan Ramey Cleveland

Senior Editor, Editorial Services: Olivia Kindig Wells

Art Director: James Boone

Great American Quilts Book Five

Editor: Carol Logan Newbill

Editorial Assistant: Cecile Y. Nierodzinski

Copy Editor: Susan S. Cheatham

Production and Distribution Director: Phillip Lee

Associate Production Manager: Theresa L. Beste

Production Assistant: Faye Porter Bonner

Associate Art Director: Cynthia R. Cooper

Designer: Larry Hunter

Patterns and Illustrations: Kelly Davis

Publishing Systems Administrator: Rick Tucker

Senior Photographer: John O'Hagan

Photo Stylist: Linda Baltzell Wright

EDITOR'S NOTE

When we ask quiltmakers what attracts them to quilts, the answer we hear most often is *color!* In celebration of color, as well as motion and design, we offer six beautiful quilts in our special chapter "Color Dance." Sandra Torguson based her quilt *Midnight Dance* on a block called Bolero, designed in honor of two extraordinary ice dancers. And Jennie Lahring's *Pineapple Colorwheel,* done in primary and secondary hues, would make a wonderful color reference for your sewing room wall.

What could be more American than cows and barns? "Quilts Across America" features them both: Rita Shatley's *Barns* and Peg Voll's *Cow Quilt.* And fans of antique-style appliqué quilts will enjoy making Darlene Christopherson's *Peacock Medallion.*

"Traditions in Quilting" includes quilts for those who like to piece as well as those who enjoy appliqué. Margaret Gulledge's *Jamie's Texas Star,* made for the youngest of her four granddaughters, combines appliquéd flowers with six-pointed Texas Stars in a lovely, old-fashioned quilt. And from a quilter named Starr Howell, we include a quilt called *Twirling Stars.*

We complete this collection of 26 quilts with the artistry showcased in "Designer Gallery," ranging from Betsy Cannon's tongue-in-cheek *Chickens Who Run with the Wolves* to Charlene Hughes's tranquil *Tadaima.*

Where do our Great American quilters come from? They come from Colorado and North Carolina, from Minnesota and Texas, from Arizona and Michigan. This year's book features quilts from quilters and quilting groups in 15 states across America.

If your state isn't represented, let us put a star on next year's map for you! For information on submitting a quilt, write to *Great American Quilts* Editor, Oxmoor House, 2100 Lakeshore Drive, Birmingham, AL 35209.

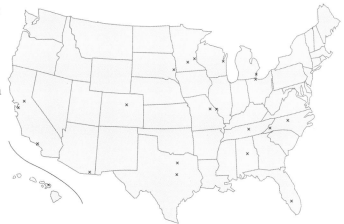

Color Dance

Quilts Across America

Traditions in Quilting

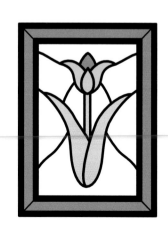

E N T S

Bee Quilters

Designer Gallery

Quilt Smart Workshop

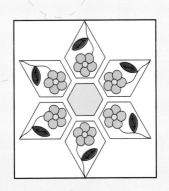

Color Dance

Jennie A. Lahring
Huachuca City, Arizona

*J*ennie Lahring's mischievous sense of humor sparkles throughout her conversation. Ask her what her occupation is, and she answers in a

"Quilting is a grand way to meet people from many places."

totally serious manner, "I'm retired from being a petroleum transfer engineer." And as you are showing how impressed you are, she grins and adds, "That's a lovely way to say I pumped full-serve gas."

It's easy to see that Jennie loves people. And although her home in the high desert country of Arizona is remote, her life is never isolated. "Quilting is a grand way to meet people from many places," Jennie says. "A friend brings a friend to see my quilts, and shortly the friend calls and wants to bring another friend. I've met people from other countries this way."

Living in the desert and being surrounded by beauty also sharpens her inner eye, Jennie says. "Before I started making quilts, I wasn't aware of what I was seeing," she says. "Now I really look at color and perspective."

Pineapple Colorwheel
1994

"I love color and like foundation piecing," Jennie says. "I wanted to do a color wheel quilt after I saw a Log Cabin-style color wheel."

Ever the "different drummer," Jennie decided to use the Pineapple pattern for her quilt because she didn't want to copy someone else's idea. She chose hand-dyed fabrics in two shades each of nine colors and set them off with stark black-and-white background strips.

"I suppose the main reason I made this quilt is the usual one," Jennie says. "I like quilts. I make quilts, and I'm not happy if I don't have several in progress at all times."

Pineapple Colorwheel

Finished Quilt Size
30" x 30"

Number of Blocks and Finished Size
9 blocks   9" x 9"

Fabric Requirements
Black print   1 yard*
Light gray print   ¾ yard
Dark gray print   ½ yard
Hand-dyed fabrics**   10" square
Backing   1 yard
*Includes fabric for binding.
**You will need 1 light and 1 dark each
of 9 colors, for a total of 18 (10")
squares of hand-dyed fabric.

Pieces to Cut
Black print
     4 (1¾" x 30½") border strips
     8 (2"-wide) crosswise strips
     12 (1"-wide) crosswise strips
Light gray print
     4 (1" x 28½") border strips
     14 (1"-wide) crosswise strips
Dark gray print
     16 (1½") squares
     12 (1"-wide) crosswise strips
Hand-dyed fabric***
     2 (1½") squares
     1 (2"-wide) crosswise strip
     2 (1"-wide) crosswise strips
***Cut these pieces from each of the 18
fabrics.

Quilt Top Assembly
1. Referring to *Quilt Smart* on pages 12–13, foundation-piece 36 quarter-blocks. You will have 2 quarter-blocks of each hand-dyed fabric.

2. Referring to *Block Assembly Diagram*, join 2 light and 2 dark quarter-blocks of each color to form 1 block. Repeat to make 9 blocks.

3. Referring to *Quilt Top Assembly Diagram*, join blocks in 3 rows of 3 blocks each.

4. Referring to photograph for placement, appliqué 1½" dark gray print squares over corners of blocks as shown.

5. Join 1"-wide light gray print borders to edges of quilt, mitering corners. Press borders away from quilt.

6. Join 1¾"-wide black print borders to edges of quilt, mitering corners. Press away from quilt.

Quilting
Quilt in-the-ditch around all pieces and borders.

Finished Edges
Bind with straight-grain or bias binding made from black print.

Quilt Top Assembly Diagram

Color Key

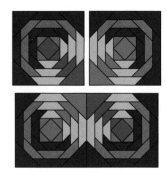

Block Assembly Diagram

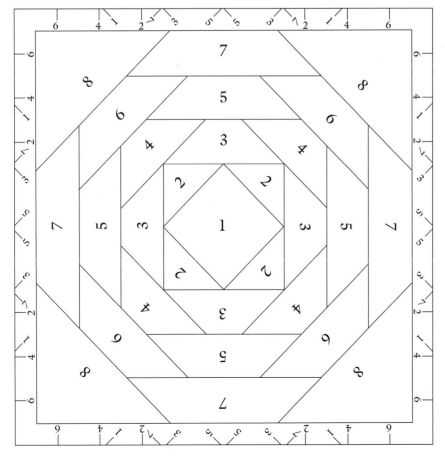

Foundation Block

Trace or photocopy this block onto tracing paper to make the foundations for paper piecing. You may make as many copies for personal use as you need.

Foundation Piecing

1. Trace or photocopy the foundation block on page 11 onto tracing paper, and trim each copy along outside lines. You will need 36 foundations to complete the quilt, but it's always a good idea to have extras in case you make a mistake. It's often easier to start over than to try to remove the small stitches without ripping the paper foundation.

2. For each quarter-block, lay out 1 (1½") square, 1 (2"-wide) strip, 1 (1"-wide) strip, 1 (1"-wide) light print strip, 1 (1"-wide) dark print strip, 1 (1"-wide) black print strip, and 1 (2"-wide) black print strip.

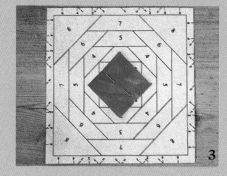

3. Place square over center square of foundation (#1). Pin in place.

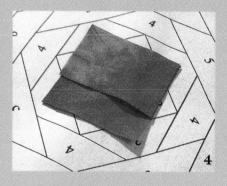

4. From 1"-wide strip, cut a 1½"-long piece. With right sides facing and raw edges aligned, place strip over one edge of square.

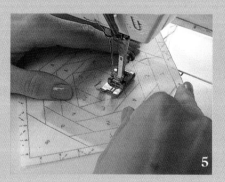

5. Set your sewing machine for a stitch length of 10–12 stitches per inch. (The tighter stitching holds the fabric more firmly and perforates the paper foundation more closely for

easier removal.) Turn foundation over. Stitch along line on foundation paper between #1 and #2, beginning and ending at edges of fabric.

6. Clip ends of threads. Turn foundation over. Using your fingers or a tool such as the hera marker shown here, press strip away from square to cover area #2.

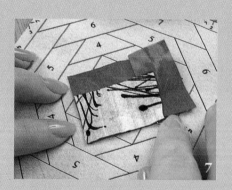

7. From light print strip, cut 3 (1½"-long) pieces. With right sides facing and raw edges aligned as shown in photograph, place one piece on square.

8. Turn foundation over. Stitch along line between #1 and #2. Clip thread ends. Press strip away from square. Repeat with remaining light strips to cover #2 areas.

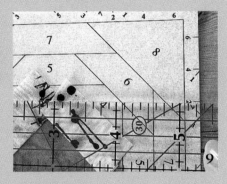

9. Align edges of ruler with marks labeled "2" on edges of foundation block.

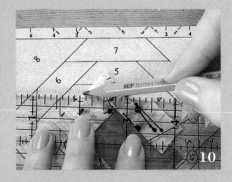

10. Draw line along edge of ruler onto fabric.

11. Trim fabric along drawn line, folding foundation paper out of the way. Do not cut through foundation paper. Repeat to trim remaining edges.

12. Cut 2 (2"-long) pieces from dark print and 2 (2"-long) pieces from black print. With right sides facing and raw edges aligned, stitch strips to block as shown to complete third row.

13. After attaching each strip, clip threads and press strip away from center. Align edges of ruler with marks labeled "3" on edges of foundation block. Draw line along edge of ruler onto fabric. Trim edges.

14. Referring to color key on page 11, complete rows 4–7 in same fashion. To complete row 8, stitch 2"-wide strips to corners as shown on color key on page 11. Turn foundation over and trim edges of fabric even with edges of block.

15. To complete quarter-block, tear away foundation, using tweezers if necessary to remove small bits. Press completed block with iron.

Joan Dyer
Redondo Beach, California

*J*oan's first exposure to quilting came in 1989, when her sister, Carol Webb, invited her to come to the big quilt show in Paducah, Kentucky. Joan, a potter, asked innocently, "What's a quilt show? Where's Paducah? What *is* quilting?"

"What's a quilt show? Where's Paducah? What is quilting?"

She learned fast. "Carol signed me up for classes with Virginia Avery and Katie Pasquini," Joan remembers. "I didn't have the sense to be intimidated and proceeded to have a fantastic time!"

Back home in California, Joan took more quilting classes, joined the South Bay Quilters Guild, and began entering her quilts in shows and submitting them to magazines.

"I've been unbelievably fortunate to find a medium in which I can achieve such satisfaction," she says. "Quilting saved me from 'empty nest syndrome' after my daughters' marriages. And it allows me to work with clean hands—no more clay and glaze under my fingernails!"

Persian Plenty
1995

Joan made *Persian Plenty* as a wedding gift for her second daughter, Kim, and her fiancé Phil Meyers. Two years before, Joan had made a dramatic Amish pinwheel quilt for the wedding of Kim's older sister, Cheryl. "I knew that the day would come when I would have to come up with an equally successful but entirely different quilt for Kim," Joan says. "When it became obvious that she had

her future husband picked out, I sat down at the computer and began to play with block designs."

Kim requested a scrap quilt and chose the color scheme of teal, purple, and butterscotch. Joan designed a simple block based on a nine-patch unit and began making block after block, using hundreds of different fabrics. "I followed my computer design for color placement as I

went," Joan says. "I didn't sew any blocks together until the entire quilt was on the design wall."

Joan emphasizes that laying out the blocks before stitching them together is crucial. "Construction is not difficult," she says, "but the color placement and setting require care."

For tips on making your own design wall, see *Quilt Smart* on page 18.

15

Persian Plenty

Finished Quilt Size
100" x 116"

Number of Blocks and Finished Size
120 blocks   8" x 8"

Fabric Requirements
Dark prints*   12 yards total

Gold prints   3¼ yards total

Backing   10½ yards

Dark green print
for binding   1 yard

*Joan used prints in dark shades of blue, green, purple, rust, and red.

Pieces to Cut
Dark prints
    1,356 (2½"-square) A
    146 B**
    146 B rev.**
    172 C***
    134 (2½" x 4½") D
    4 F
    4 F rev.
    4 G
    4 G rev.
    4 H
    4 H rev.
Gold prints
    146 B**
    146 B rev.**
    172 C***
    4 E

**See Step 1.
***To make 2 Cs, cut 1 (2⅞") square from dark print; cut in half diagonally.

Quilt Top Assembly

1. To make 2 Bs, cut 1 (2½" x 7") rectangle from dark print; cut in half diagonally from lower left to upper right. To make 2 Bs rev., cut 1 (2½" x 7") rectangle from dark print; cut in half diagonally from upper left to lower right.

2. Referring to *Block Assembly Diagram,* join 9 dark print As, 1 dark print B, 1 dark print B rev., 1 gold print B, 1 gold print B rev., 1 dark print C, and 1 gold print C as shown to make 1 block. Repeat to make 120 blocks.

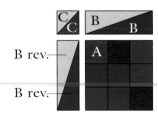

Block Assembly Diagram Make 120.

3. Referring to photograph and *Quilt Top Assembly Diagram* for color placement, arrange blocks on floor or design wall in 12 rows of 10. (See *Quilt Smart* on page 18 for tips on making design wall.) Rotate blocks as shown to create concentric pattern. When satisfied with color placement, join blocks into rows. Join rows.

4. Cut remaining dark print fabric into 2½" squares, 2½" x 4½" rectangles, and 2½" x 6½" rectangles.

5. To make dark pieced inner border for top of quilt, randomly join dark print squares and rectangles to make 80½"-long pieced strip. Join to top of

quilt. Repeat to make and join dark pieced inner border for bottom of quilt.

6. Referring to *Border Block 1 Assembly Diagram,* join 1 dark print B, 1 dark print B rev., 1 gold print B, 1 gold print B rev., 2 dark print Cs, and 2 gold print Cs as shown to make 1 Border Block 1.

Border Block 1 Assembly Diagram
Make 2.

7. To make dark pieced inner border for 1 side of quilt, randomly join dark print squares and rectangles to make 2 (42½"-long) pieced strips. Join 1 pieced strip to each end of Border Block 1. Join border to 1 side of quilt, butting corners.

8. Repeat Steps 6 and 7 to make and join second side pieced inner border.

9. Referring to *Border Block 2 Assembly Diagram,* join 6 dark print As, 1 dark print B, 1 dark print B rev., 1 gold print B, 1 gold print B rev., and 6 dark print Ds as shown to make 1 Border Block 2. Repeat to make 22 blocks.

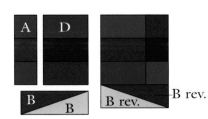

Border Block 2 Assembly Diagram
Make 22.

10. Referring to *Border Block 3 Assembly Diagram,* join 6 dark

print As, 2 dark print Cs, and 2 gold print Cs as shown to make 1 Border Block 3. Repeat to make 24 blocks.

Border Block 3 Assembly Diagram
Make 24.

11. Referring to *Border Block 4 Assembly Diagram,* join 1 dark

print B, 1 dark print B rev., 1 gold print B, 1 gold print B rev., and 1 dark print D as shown to make 1 Border Block 4. Repeat to make 2 blocks.

Border Block 4 Assembly Diagram
Make 2.

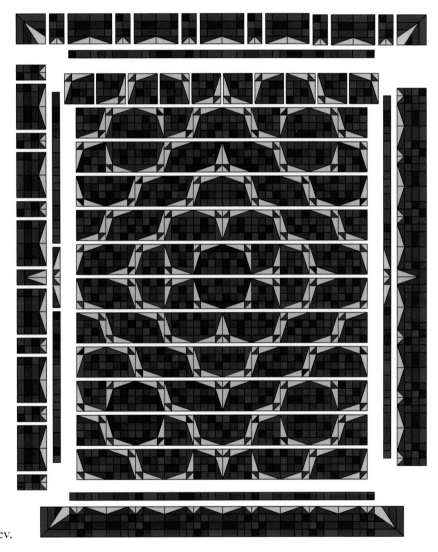

Quilt Top Assembly Diagram

12. Referring to *Corner Block Assembly Diagram,* join 1 gold print E, 1 dark print F, 1 dark print F rev., 1 dark print G, 1 dark print G rev., 1 dark print H, and 1 dark print H rev. as shown to make 1 Corner Block. Repeat to make 4 blocks.

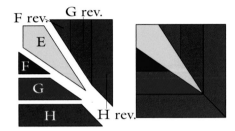

Corner Block Assembly Diagram Make 4.

13. To make 1 side pieced outer border, join 6 Border Block 2s, 6 Border Block 3s, and 1 Border Block 4 as shown in *Quilt Top Assembly Diagram.* Join to 1 side of quilt.

14. Repeat to make and join second side pieced outer border.

15. To make top pieced outer border, join 2 Corner Blocks, 5 Border Block 2s, and 6 Border Block 3s as shown in *Quilt Top Assembly Diagram.* Join to top of quilt.

16. Repeat to make and join bottom pieced outer border.

Quilting

Quilt in-the-ditch around all pieces and borders, or quilt as desired.

Finished Edges

Bind with straight-grain or bias binding made from dark green print.

❖ QUILT SMART ❖

Design Wall

To duplicate the color grouping used in Joan's quilt, you will need to arrange all of the blocks before joining them. However, providing a space large enough for the entire quilt top without having the pieces stepped on and scattered by children or pets can be a problem. Professional quilters often dedicate a wall in their studios for this purpose, paneling it with cork or bulletin board material and then pinning the pieces directly to the wall as the design proceeds. If you don't have the luxury of a dedicated design wall, make a temporary design board to use instead.

Flannel sheet: If you have an empty wall space measuring approximately 7' wide x 8' high, the least expensive design board may not be a board at all. Buy approximately 5 yards of flannel, felt, or polyester fleece (such as Thermolam). Cut it into two lengths of 90" each and stitch them together to make one large sheet measuring about 88" x 90". Pin the sheet to the wall along the top edge. As you place each block, smooth it against the fabric; the block will cling to the fuzzy surface. When you are pleased with the arrangement, pin the blocks to the flannel for more security. The sheet can be taken down and rolled up, pins and all, until you are ready to join the blocks.

Free-standing board: If you don't have enough empty wall space, you will need to construct a free-standing board measuring at least 85" x 90" to accommodate all the blocks for the quilt top. If you have room for it, a longer board will be more comfortable to use; you won't be forced to place pieces all the way to the floor. But don't buy a board longer than 92" unless you have high ceilings in your workroom.

Artist's foam-core board, available from art supply and some office supply stores in sheets up to 48" x 96", is an ideal material to use because it is lightweight and easy to pin. Buy two sheets and trim each to the best length for your space. To hinge the sheets, cut a strip of muslin 4" wide by the length you have chosen. Place the foam-core sheets on the floor, butting long edges. Glue the muslin strip to each sheet, centering the strip over the "seam" line. Let the glue dry and stand the board upright. The hinge allows you to fold the board slightly, like a screen, if it must stand by itself. Or lean it against a wall, desk, or other piece of furniture for a flat surface. If you wish, cover the foam core with flannel, felt, or fleece to enable you to temporarily place your pieces as described above. Or leave the foam core uncovered and pin each piece directly to the board as you place it.

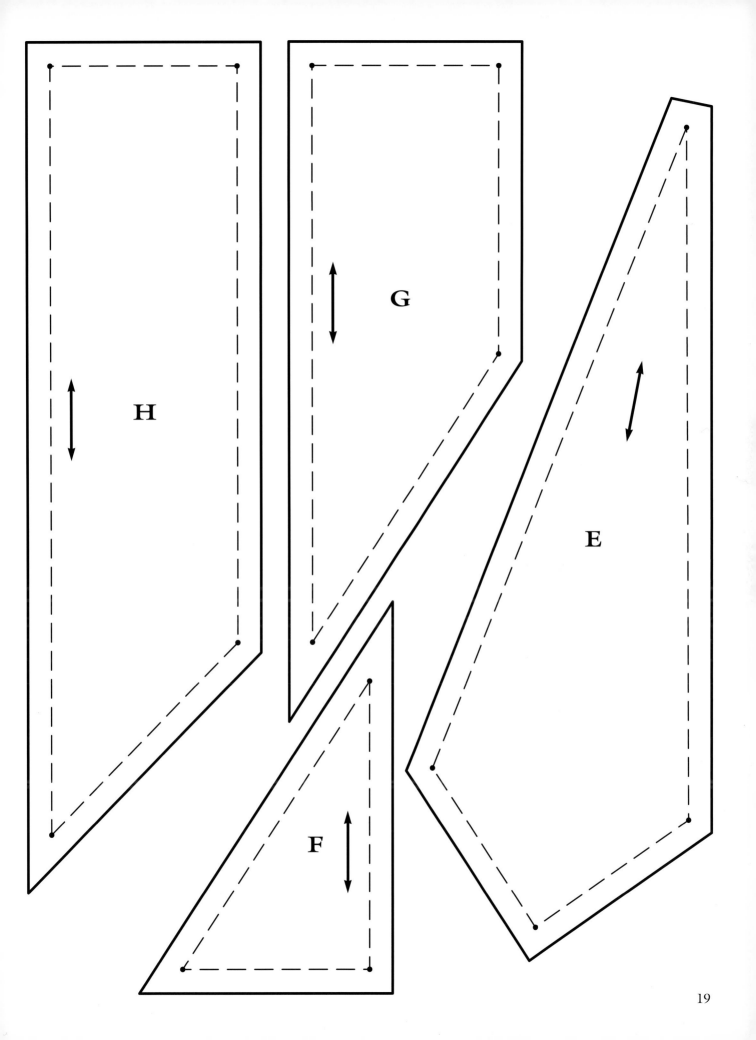

H

G

E

F

Rebecca Rohrkaste
Berkeley, California

*R*ebecca Rohrkaste leads a very colorful life—at least as far as her quilting is concerned! "Choosing colors and fabrics and manipulating them are the most exciting part of quilting for me," says Rebecca. "I want the fabric color and arrangement to be interesting, original, and somewhat unexpected. My quilts range from reinterpretations of traditional designs and techniques to more contemporary quilts with a painterly emphasis on color and color relationships." It's not surprising that Rebecca views her quilts with an artist's eye. She majored in sculpture at Rhode Island School of Design and has continued her art studies at both Carnegie-Mellon University and Penland School of Crafts. Since Rebecca took her first quilting class in 1977, quilting has become not only an outlet for her creative, artistic nature, but also a means by which she has developed many friendships. "Quilting has given me a refuge, a challenge, and a source of close friends."

> *"When designing quilts, I'm very conscious of how simple, repeated geometric forms play off the complex emotional effects of color and fabric."*

Sparks: July
1995

When Rebecca saw a version of this tipped star block at an international quilt show in 1993, she and several of her friends presented it as a "challenge" block to their quilt group. During a quilting weekend, four members of the group, including Rebecca, chose to work on the challenge block. "I made many of the stars that weekend, and then put them aside for quite a while because they weren't working for me," she says. In the summer of 1995 she pulled them out again. She eliminated some of the blocks, made some new ones, and reworked others so that they would be a bit more irregular. "The blocks look like fireworks, or sparklers, or hot dancing summer stars," Rebecca says. "And because I stitched on the quilt over the 4th of July, the quilt became *Sparks: July.*"

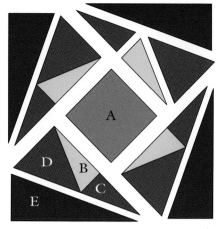

Block Assembly Diagram

2. Join blocks in 6 rows of 5 blocks each, as shown in *Quilt Top Assembly Diagram.*

3. Join rows.

Quilting

Quilt in-the-ditch around all pieces, or quilt as desired.

Finished Edges

Bind with straight-grain or bias binding made from purple.

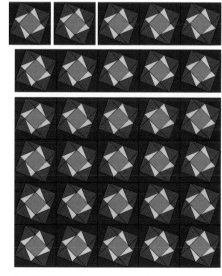

Quilt Top Assembly Diagram

Sparks: July

Finished Quilt Size
60" x 72"

Number of Blocks and Finished Size
30 blocks   12" x 12"

Fabric Requirements

Orange plaids
  and prints   1 yard
                     total
Gold prints   1 yard
                     total
Purple plaids
  and prints   1 yard
                     total
Dark prints   1 yard
                     total

Backing   4½ yards
Purple for binding   ¾ yard

Pieces to Cut
Orange plaids and prints
  30 A
Gold prints
  120 B
Purple plaids and prints*
  120 C
  120 D
Dark prints
  120 E
*Cut 1 C and 1 D of each plaid or print.

Quilt Top Assembly
1. Referring to *Block Assembly Diagram,* join 1 A, 4 Bs, 4 Cs, 4 Ds, and 4 Es as shown to make 1 block. Repeat to make 30 blocks.

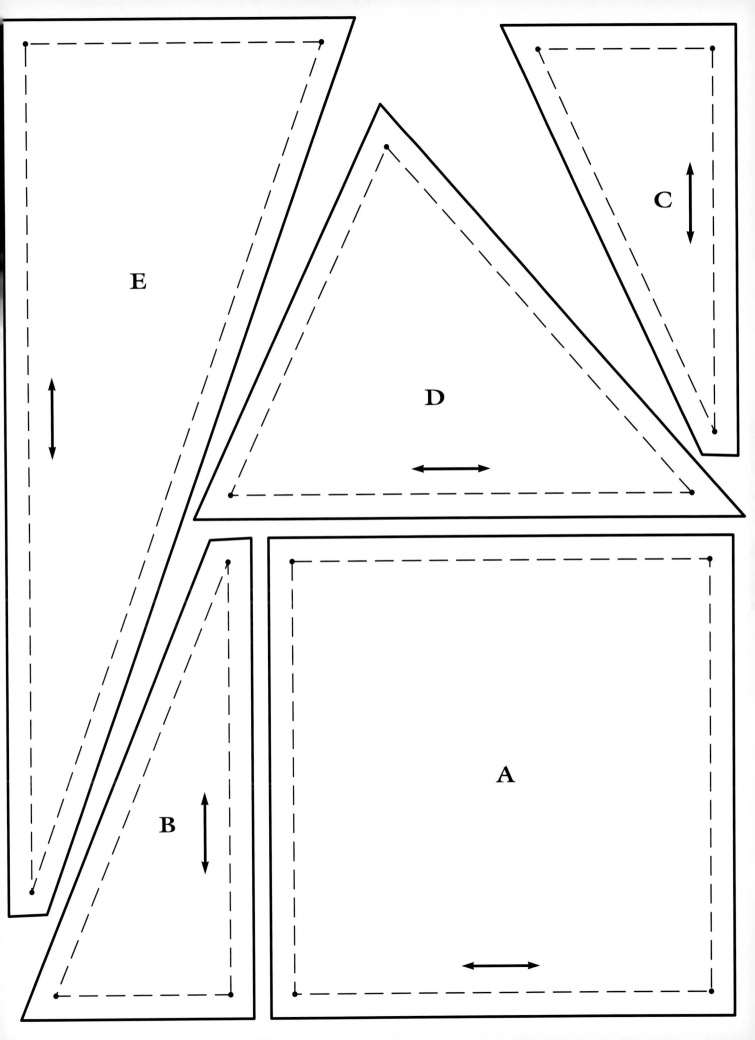

E

C

D

A

B

Sandra Torguson
Sacramento, California

$\mathcal{A}$lthough Sandra Torguson learned to sew as a child, she chose a different creative path as an adult, becoming a professional calligrapher and instructor.

"I worked with paper and pens and appreciated the artistic freedom, but I finally realized that I missed the feel of fabric," says Sandra. "So I began taking quilting classes and joined River City Quilters Guild." She was immediately fascinated with how no two quilts looked the same. "Each quilter added her own magic," she says. "Color and designs danced before me."

Sandra is now trying to find a way to combine both of her loves into a single whole. "Surface design is another aspect of quilting that I hope to pursue," she says. "I want to include my lettering with quilting. Along with two other calligraphers, I am planning a calligraphy show without limits. A quilt or two may very well be part of the exhibition!"

Midnight Dance
1996

During a vacation, Sandra wanted to work on a challenging hand-piecing project.

"This 52-piece block, complete with curves, was my choice," says Sandra. The quilt block, "Bolero," appeared in *Quilter's Newsletter Magazine* and honors ice dancers Jayne Torvill and Christopher Dean, whose dance routine to Ravel's *Bolero* has become a signature piece for them.

As Sandra assembled the quilt, she decided to emphasize color as a unifying factor in a busy design. "The off-white fabric that appears in all the blocks establishes unity," she says. "The main colors are complimentary in each block. And I reuse one of the fabrics in each block in another block." The border colors and fabric designs continue the "dance." The blocks are hand pieced, the border is machine pieced, and the entire quilt is machine quilted.

Midnight Dance

Finished Quilt Size
56" x 56"

Number of Blocks and Finished Size

9 blocks   12" x 12"

Fabric Requirements

White print	1¼ yards
Black	1 yard
Black/white stripe I	½ yard
Black/white stripe II	⅜ yard
Red/turquoise print	¼ yard
Red	¼ yard
Turquoise	¼ yard
Blue	¼ yard
Purple	¼ yard
Light prints	½ yard total
Dark prints	½ yard total
Backing	3½ yards
Black for binding	¾ yard

Pieces to Cut

White
    72 A
    36 B rev.
    72 C
    36 F
    36 G
Black
    122 (2½") squares
    24 (2½" x 4½") rectangles
Black/white stripe I
    8 (1½" x 40½") border strips
Black/white stripe II
    40 (2½") squares
    12 (¾" x 12½") sashing strips
Red/turquoise print
    48 (2½") squares
Red
    16 (2½") squares
    6 (2½" x 4½") rectangles

Turquoise
    16 (2½") squares
    6 (2½" x 4½") rectangles
Blue
    4 (2½") sashing squares
    5 (1½" x 12½") sashing strips
Purple
    9 (1½" x 12½") sashing strips
Light prints*
    36 A rev.
    72 D
    36 D rev.
Dark prints*
    144 B
    36 B rev.
    36 C
    36 E
*See Step 1 before cutting.

Quilt Top Assembly

1. To simplify block construction, sort pieces for each block into separate piles; pin together or place into plastic bags. For each block, you should have the following pieces:

White: 8 As, 4 Bs rev., 8 Cs, 4 Fs, and 4 Gs.

First light print: 4 As rev.

Second light print: 8 Ds and 4 Ds rev.

First dark print: 8 Bs and 4 Cs.

Second dark print: 8 Bs, 4 Bs rev., and 4 Es.

2. Referring to *Block Assembly Diagram*, join pieces as shown to form 1 block. Repeat to make 9 blocks.

3. To make 1 sashing strip, join 2 (1½" x 12½") sashing strips of different colors to each side of 1 (¾" x 12½") black/white stripe II strip.

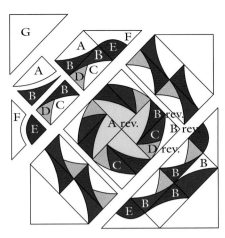

Block Assembly Diagram

(Refer to photograph for color placement.) Repeat to make 12 sashing strips.

4. To make 1 block row, alternately join 3 blocks and 2 sashing strips, as shown in *Quilt Top Assembly Diagram*. Repeat to make 3 block rows.

5. To make 1 sashing row, alternately join 3 sashing strips and 2 (2½") blue squares, as shown in *Quilt Top Assembly Diagram*.

6. Alternately join block rows and sashing rows.

7. To make inner top border, join 2 (1½" x 40½") black/white stripe I strips along long edges. Join to top of quilt. Repeat to make and join inner bottom border.

8. To make 1 inner side border, join 2 (1½" x 40½") black/white stripe I strips along long edges. Join 1 (2½") black square to each end of border. Join to 1 side of quilt, butting corners. Repeat to make and join second inner side border.

9. To make 1 outer side border, join 10 black/white stripe II squares, 10 red/turquoise print squares, 6 turquoise squares, 3 turquoise rectangles, 22 black squares, and 6 black rectangles as shown in *Quilt Top Assembly Diagram*. Join to 1 side of quilt. Repeat to make and join second outer side border.

10. To make outer top border, join 10 black/white stripe II squares, 14 red/turquoise print squares, 2 turquoise squares, 8 red squares, 3 red rectangles, 32 black squares, and 6 black rectangles as shown in *Quilt Top Assembly Diagram*. Join to top of quilt. Repeat to make and join outer bottom border.

Quilting

Quilt in-the-ditch around all pieces. Quilt crosshatch pattern across border squares and rectangles, or quilt as desired.

Finished Edges

Bind with straight-grain or bias binding made from black.

Quilt Top Assembly Diagram

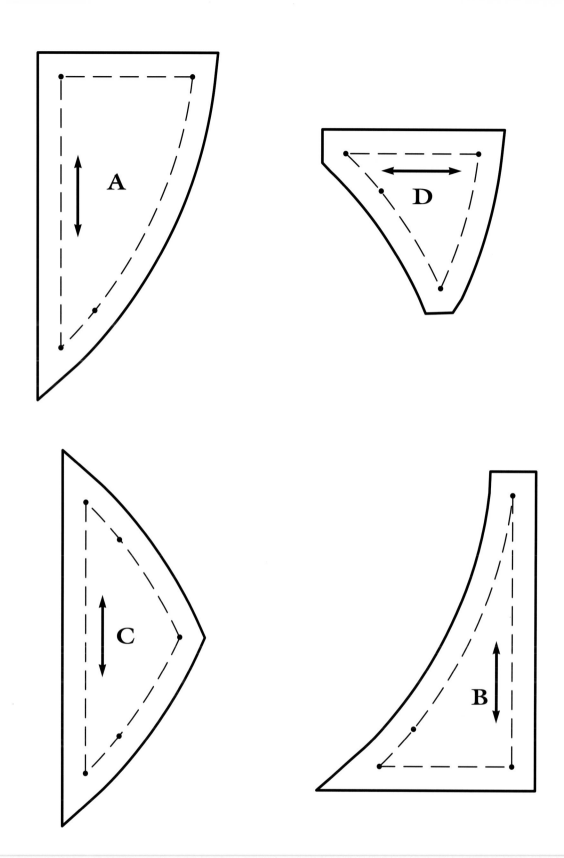

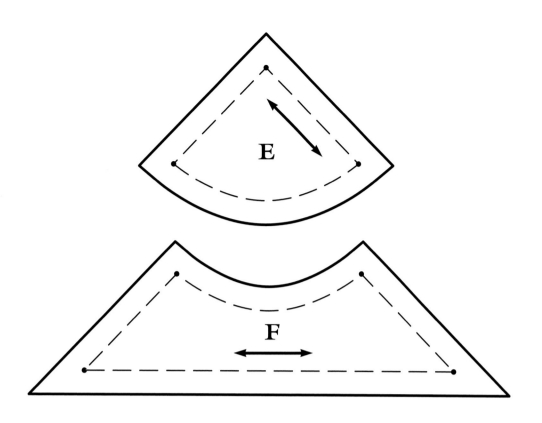

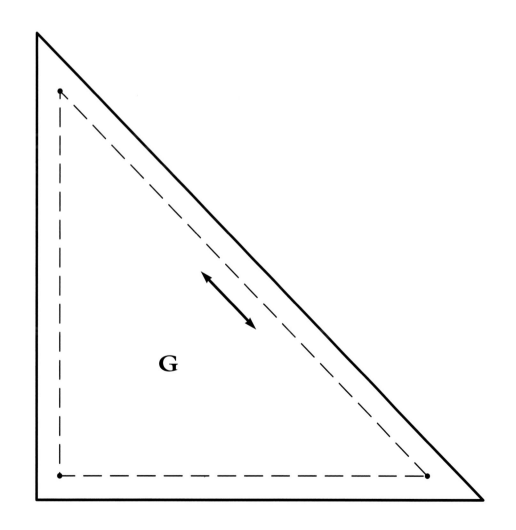

29

Kay Anderson
Waco, Texas

*I*n 1988, Kay Anderson and her sister took a log cabin quilt class, and Kay was immediately hooked! "I never really liked handwork, so I was surprised when I took to hand quilting," says Kay. "It has been great therapy for me and has helped me through some difficult times."

> *"When I get the blues, I just go to my sewing room and the blues are soon forgotten!"*

A serious illness meant that, before she received a lung transplant in 1995, Kay needed oxygen to ease her breathing. "I would have to rest and pace myself, but I hated just sitting and doing nothing," she says. "Quilting saved my sanity, because although I was still taking it easy, I was accomplishing something at the same time." Kay is doing very well today. But if she ever gets down, she says she knows just the remedy. "Whenever I get the blues, I can go to my sewing room, start cutting and piecing, and those blues are soon forgotten."

My Stained-Glass Window
1995

Like many quilts, Kay's *Stained-Glass Window* had its beginnings in a guild project. In 1992, the members of the Homespun Quilters Guild talked about making a "time capsule" quilt. Each member would make a block from the same pattern, and the blocks would be put in a box to be stored for a number of years before the quilt was completed.

"We never followed through with the idea," Kay says, "but I liked the block we chose and thought that I should make a quilt from it."

Kay, a confessed "fabriholic," says she really enjoyed pulling the many fabrics to make the quilt.

"I completed it in 1995 and had planned to enter it in our guild show that August," she says. "But I had surgery in June of that year and didn't quite have the quilting finished." We'll expect to see it in the show this year, Kay!

My Stained-Glass Window

Finished Quilt Size
83¼" x 83¼"

Number of Blocks and Finished Size
21 blocks   12" x 12"

Fabric Requirements

Black	3 yards
Floral prints	1¼ yards
Light prints	1¼ yards
Medium prints	1½ yards
Dark prints	1 yard
Background print	1¼ yards
Backing	1 yard
Black for binding	1 yard

Pieces to Cut

Black
- 2 (1" x 79¼") border strips
- 2 (2" x 76¼") border strips
- 4 (1" x 29") border strips
- 12 (2" x 26½") sashing strips
- 16 (1" x 12½") sashing strips
- 8 (1" x 13") sashing strips

Floral prints
- 4 (1¾" x 15") border strips
- 4 (4" square) border As

Light prints
- 2 (11⅛") squares*

Medium prints
- 6 (4" x 7⅜") rectangles

Dark prints
- 6 (4" x 7⅜") rectangles

Background print
- 2 (21") squares*
- 2 (19") squares**

*Cut each square in half diagonally for 2 corner triangles.
**Cut each square into quarters diagonally for 4 side triangles.

Quilt Top Assembly

1. For 1 block, cut 8 (2" x 5½") rectangles of same medium print. From black, cut 8 (¾" x 5½") and 8 (¾" x 2") strips. Join 1 short black strip to short edge of 1 rectangle. Join 1 long black strip to adjacent long edge of rectangle. Press seam allowances toward strips. Repeat for all 8 print rectangles.

2. To make 1 block, cut the following pieces. From floral print: 1 (4"-square) A, 4 (2¼"-square) Es, and 4 (2"-square) Hs. From dark print: 4 (2¼" x 4") Cs. From black: 2 (1" x 4") Bs, 2 (1" x 8½") Ds, 4 (1" x 2¼") Fs, and 4 (¾" x 9") Gs. From light print: 2 (3⅞") squares, cut in half diagonally to make 4 Is.

Join with pieced rectangles made in Step 1, trimming ends

of rectangles, as shown in *Block Assembly Diagram*.

3. Repeat Steps 1 and 2 to make 21 blocks.

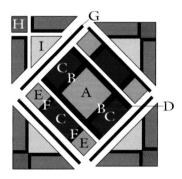

Block Assembly Diagram

4. To make center medallion, join floral print border strips to edges of 1 block, mitering corners. Join 1 light print corner triangle to each side.

Join 1 dark print rectangle to each end of 1 medium print rectangle. Join to 1 edge of medallion. Repeat for opposite edge.

Join 1 medium print rectangle to each end of 1 dark print rectangle. Join 1 A to each end of strip. Stitch to 1 side of medallion, butting corners. Repeat for opposite side.

Join 1" x 29" black border strips to edges of medallion, mitering corners.

5. To make 1 Small Corner Unit, join 4 blocks, 4 (1" x 12½") black strips, 3 (2" x 26½") black strips, and 1 background print corner triangle as shown in *Small Corner Unit Assembly Diagram*. Repeat to make 2.

6. To make 1 Large Corner Unit, join 6 blocks, 4 (1" x 12½") black strips, 3 (2" x 26½") black strips, 4 (1" x 13") black strips, 1 background print corner triangle, and 4 background print side triangles as shown in *Large Corner Unit Assembly Diagram*. Repeat to make 2.

7. Join Corner Units to center medallion as shown in *Quilt Top Assembly Diagram*.

8. Join 2" x 76¼" black strips to top and bottom of quilt. Join 1" x 79¼" black strips to sides of quilt, butting corners.

9. To make pieced borders, cut leftover prints into 2" squares and 2" x 4½" rectangles. Cut remaining black into ¾" x 2½" strips. Join squares and rectangles randomly, with 1 black strip between each print piece, to make 2 (79¼"-long) and 2 (83¼"-long) pieced borders. Join short borders to opposite sides of quilt. Join long borders

Quilt Top Assembly Diagram

to top and bottom of quilt, butting corners.

Quilting

Quilt in-the-ditch around all pieces. Quilt side and corner tri-angles with 1" cross-hatching, or quilt as desired.

Finished Edges

Bind with straight-grain or bias binding made from black.

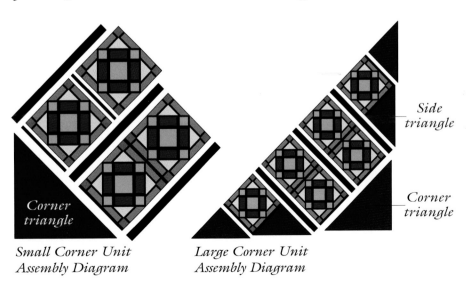

Small Corner Unit Assembly Diagram

Large Corner Unit Assembly Diagram

Sharon Chambers
Mesquite, Texas

*S*haron Chambers says she spent a lot of years as a "closet quilter."

"I had always sewed for my children," she says, "and one day my husband asked why didn't I make a quilt with all those scraps I had left over." Because there were no quilters in her family, Sharon went to the library and checked out some books on quilting. "I was really on my own," she says. "I had no idea there was this whole quilt world out there!"

"I have a headset for my phone—everyone needs one. Just clip it over your head and talk while you're sewing!"

One autumn in the early 1980s, Sharon went to Houston to visit her sister and took along some of her piecework. "My sister told me about this quilt show in town, so we decided to go see it," she says. "That quilt show" turned out to be the American International Quilt Festival, one of the largest annual exhibitions of quilts and quilting vendors in the world. "I've never looked back," Sharon says. "I've got so many quilt friends now who start their sentences with 'Sharon, why don't you try . . .?' And that's all it takes. I do!"

Ice Crystals
1996

"I love quilts that are a little out of the ordinary," Sharon says. "That's why I asked my friend Rita Runquist, a member of my quilting bee, to design a challenging quilt block for me."

Sharon likes to hand-piece and carries a small zip-top plastic bag full of quilt pieces everywhere. "I work for the Census Bureau, and I spend a lot of time waiting for people," she says. "I just pull out my little bag and stitch away. When you spend a few minutes here and there, you soon find you've managed a couple of hours on a quilt every day!"

The "Ice Crystals" block, with its many points and bias edges, presented a particular piecing challenge, even for Sharon. "I hand-pieced those rows together to get the points to match the first time I sewed it," she says. "I'm in too much of a hurry to do it by machine and have to rip it out!"

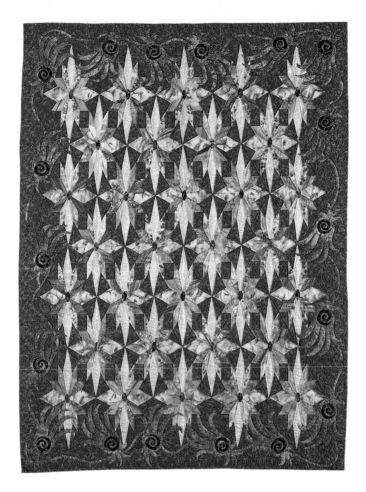

Green print
  18 I
Purple
  18 (4") squares
Brown print
  32 H

*Cut each in half diagonally for 2 corner triangles.
**For each block, cut 2 Cs and 2 Cs rev. from 1 pink print.
†For each block, cut 2 Ds and 2 Ds rev. from 1 blue print.

Quilt Top Assembly

1. Referring to *Block Assembly Diagram,* join 2 As, 2 Bs, 2 Bs rev., 2 Cs, 2 Cs rev., 2 Ds, 2 Ds rev., 2 Es, 2 Es rev., 2 Fs, 2 Gs, and 2 Gs rev. as shown. To complete block, appliqué 1 H over center. Repeat to make 32 blocks.

Ice Crystals

Finished Quilt Size
68½" x 88½"

Number of Blocks and Finished Size
32 blocks   12" x 20"

Fabric Requirements

Red print	6½ yards
Gray print I	1½ yards
Gray print II	1½ yards
Pink prints	1¾ yards total
Blue prints	1½ yards total
Green print	2½ yards
Purple print	¼ yard
Brown print	¼ yard
Backing	5½ yards
Purple for binding	¾ yard

Pieces to Cut

Red print
  2 (4¾" x 80½") borders
  2 (4¾" x 69½") borders
  2 (6¾" x 11⅛") rectangles*
  6 (6½" x 21⅞") rectangles
  8 (10¾" x 12⅞") rectangles
  64 B
  64 B rev.
  64 E
  64 E rev.
  64 G
  64 G rev.

Gray print I
  64 A

Gray print II
  64 F

Pink prints**
  64 C
  64 C rev.

Blue prints†
  64 D
  64 D rev.

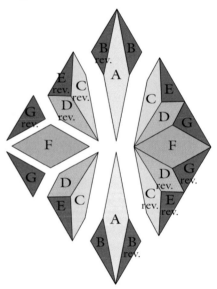

Block Assembly Diagram

2. To make 1 side triangle, fold 1 (6½" x 21⅞") red print rectangle in half; crease to mark midpoint of 1 long side. Trim as shown in *Side Triangle Cutting Diagram.* Repeat to make 6 side triangles.

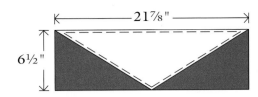

Side Triangle Cutting Diagram

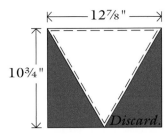

Top/Bottom Triangle Cutting Diagram

3. To make 1 top/bottom triangle, fold 1 (12⅞" x 10¾") red print rectangle in half; crease to mark midpoint of 1 long side. Trim as shown in *Top/Bottom Triangle Cutting Diagram*. Repeat to make 8 top/bottom triangles.

4. Join blocks, side triangles, top/bottom triangles, and corner triangles in diagonal rows as shown in *Quilt Top Assembly Diagram*. Join rows.

5. Join 4¾" x 80½" red print borders to sides of quilt. Join 4¾" x 69½" red print borders to top and bottom of quilt, butting corners.

6. To make 1 palm leaf for border, baste 1 purple square, right side down, to wrong side of 1 I, centering square over area to be reverse-appliquéd. Reverse-appliqué spiral shape, following instructions in *Quilt Smart* on page 38. Repeat to make 18 palm leaves.

7. From remaining green print, make 300" of ⅞"-wide bias for stems. Referring to photograph for placement, arrange palm leaves and bias stems on border of quilt. When satisfied with placement, appliqué in place.

Quilting

Quilt ¼" inside seam lines on all blocks. Quilt in-the-ditch around appliquéd leaves and stems. Quilt border and background in random swirl pattern, or quilt as desired.

Finished Edges

Bind with straight-grain or bias binding made from purple.

Quilt Top Assembly Diagram

Reverse Appliqué

1. Mark the seam lines of the spiral on the right side of one palm leaf. Center one purple square over the marked spiral.

4. On the right side of the palm leaf, baste around the marked spiral, about ¼" *outside* the seam line, as shown. Be sure to baste the inside of the spiral as well as the outside.

6. Using the point of the needle, turn the edge of the top fabric under to marked line, revealing the purple fabric underneath. Appliqué the edges, removing basting stitches as needed in tight areas.

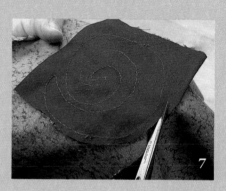

2. Mark the edges of the square with pins. Remove the square.

5. With sharp scissors, carefully trim away the top fabric about ¼" *inside* the marked seam line. Clip curves and points.

7. When the appliqué is completed, remove remaining basting stitches. Turn the leaf to the wrong side and cut away the excess purple fabric.

3. Turn the palm leaf over. On the wrong side of the leaf, center the purple square, *right side down*, aligning the edges with the pins. Pin the square to the palm leaf. Turn the leaf to the right side and remove the marking pins.

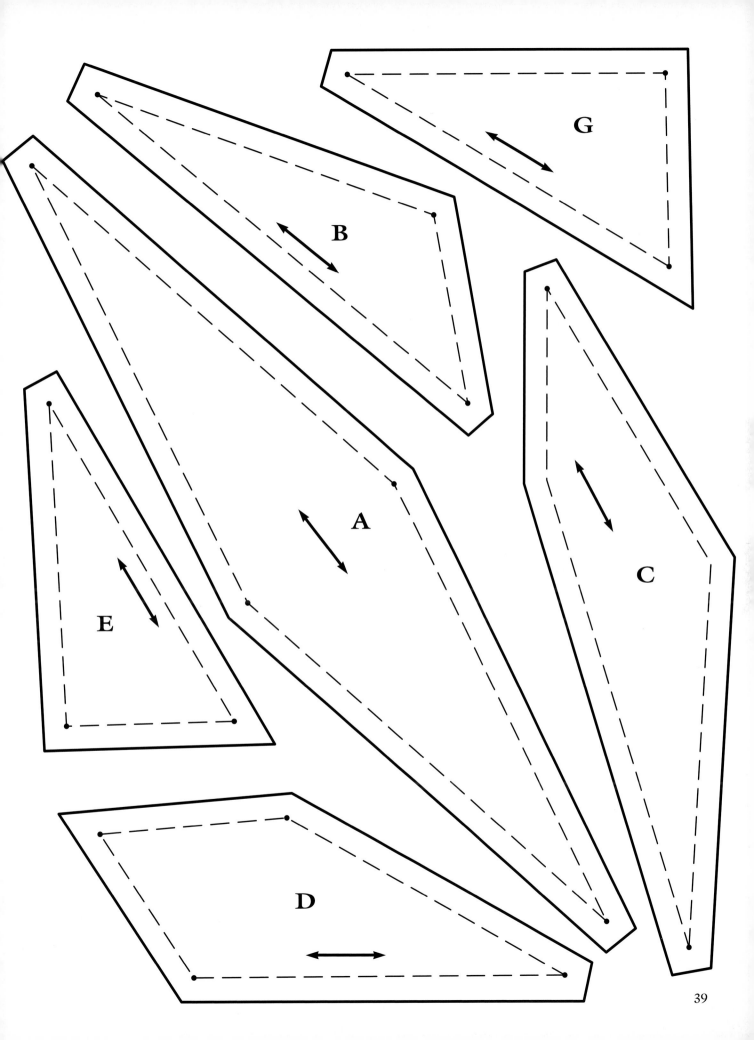

G

B

A

C

E

D

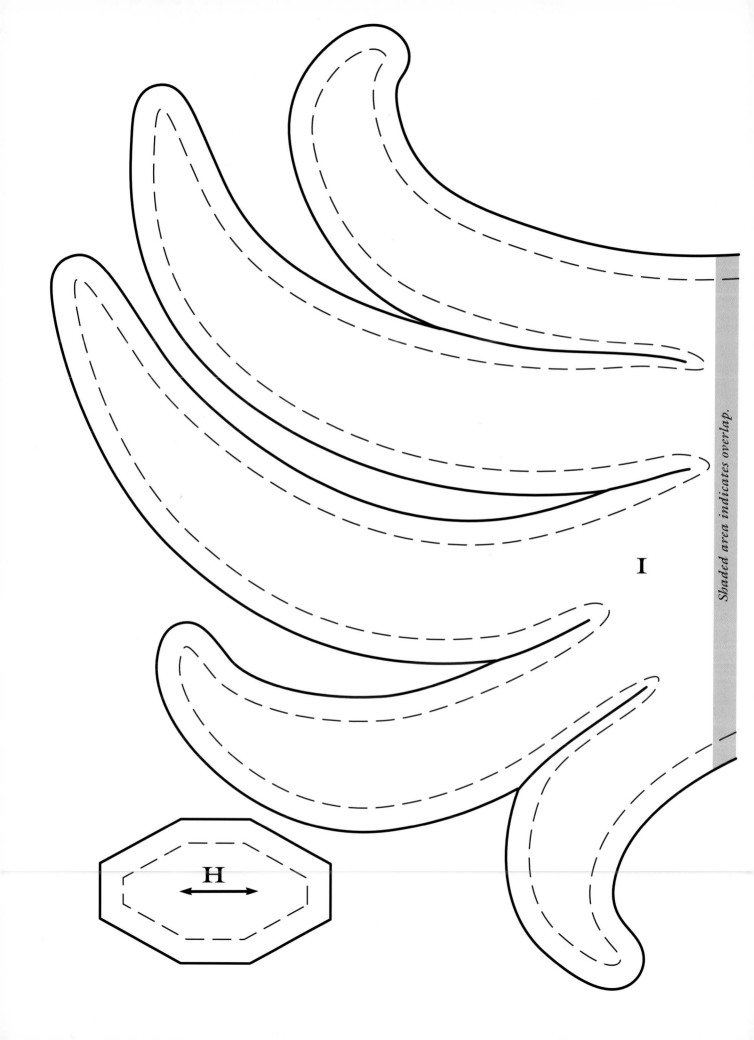

Shaded area indicates overlap.

I

H

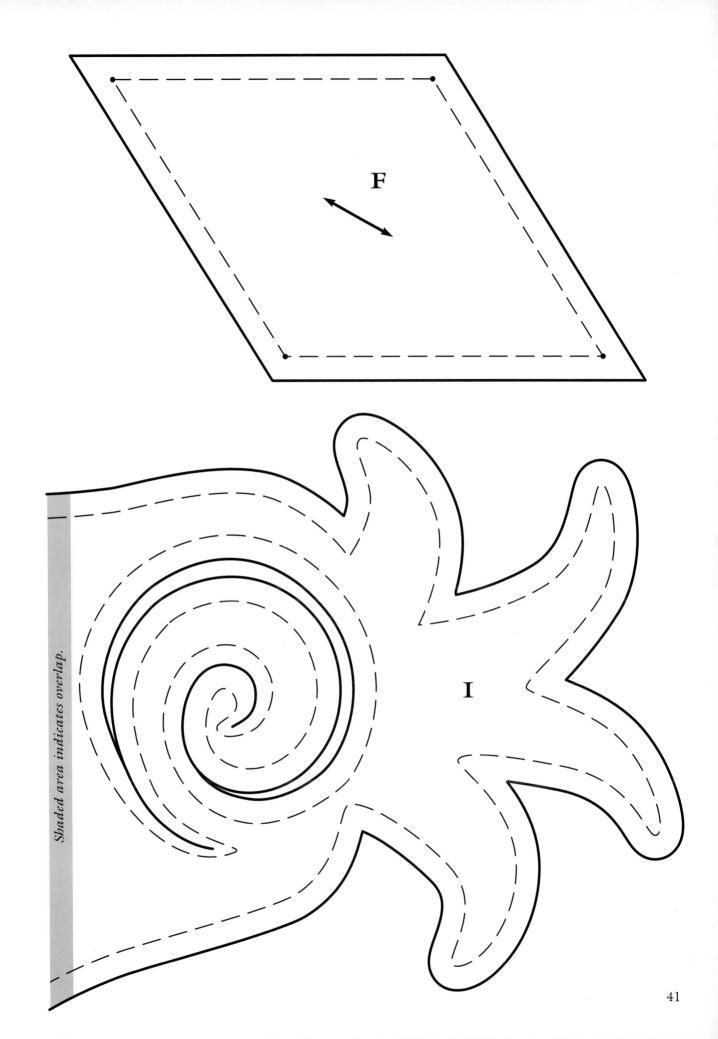

F

I

41

Quilts Across America

Barns

Charade

The Cow Quilt

Peacock Medallion

Rita Neaves Shatley
Oxford, North Carolina

"One of my most prized possessions is a quilt that my great-grandmother made, given to me by my grandmother," says Rita Shatley. "I make quilts to pass on to my own children and grandchildren—a tangible expression of the past."

"I make quilts like my grandmothers before me— for practicality and for the need to create something beautiful."

Rita feels that passing this part of her family heritage to her descendants is one of the most important things she can do. "I make quilts to leave a message to a generation not yet born," she says, "family members I will never know, but who I can touch with a part of myself." Rita's hope is that even in many years to come, her quilts will encourage, cheer, challenge, and warm the hearts of those she loves.

Barns
1995

"I grew up in the North Carolina mountains, on a farm where barns were an important part of our lives," says Rita. "When I think of a barn, it brings back vivid memories of a hard but happy childhood."

Rita made *Barns* for her daughter Sarah. Mother and daughter worked together to pick out the scraps used to make the quilt. In the border, below the bottom row of barns, she quilted a quotation from the Book of Proverbs that could be said to represent Rita's own quilting talents: "Honor the Lord with your wealth . . . then your barns will be filled to overflowing."

Barns is Rita's adaptation of a pattern called "Old McDonald's Farm" that appeared in *More Lap Quilting with Georgia Bonesteel* (Oxmoor House, 1985).

Notice the clever quilting designs Rita incorporated into the skies of her blocks. Some blocks have sunshine, while others have rain or puffy cumulus clouds. There's even a rainbow quilted into one stormy sky!

Barns

Finished Quilt Size

94½" x 115½"

Number of Blocks and Finished Size

20 blocks   21" x 21"

Fabric Requirements

Cow print	3½ yards
White	1¼ yards
Prints for sky	20 fat quarters*
Scraps	3¾ yards total
Backing	9 yards**
White for binding	¾ yard

*A fat quarter measures 18" x 22". If buying yardage, buy ⅜ yard of each sky print.
**Or 3¾ yards of 108"-wide backing fabric.

Pieces to Cut

Cow print
    2 (5¾" x 84½") border strips
    2 (5¾" x 116") border strips
White
    1,600" of 1"-wide bias strip
Prints for sky***
Scraps***
***See *Quilt Smart* on page 47.

Quilt Top Assembly

1. Referring to *Block Assembly Diagram,* join pieces as shown to make 1 block. Appliqué 1" x 6" scrap strips as shown in photograph to make windmill supports.

Repeat to make 20 blocks.

2. Join blocks in 5 rows of 4 blocks each.

3. To make top border, fold 1 (5¾" x 84½") cow print strip in half; finger-press to mark center. From center line, measure and mark "fencepost" locations every 10½" to ends of border.

From white bias, cut 16 (12"-long) strips and 7 (5¾"-long) strips. Appliqué 12"-long

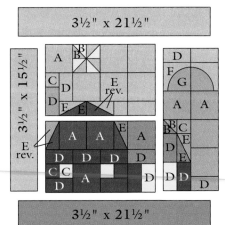

Block Assembly Diagram

strips in crisscross fashion across border as shown in photograph. Beginning at the center, appliqué 5¾"-long strips across border to make fenceposts, covering raw edges of diagonal strips. (*Note:* You will add fenceposts to end of row after you complete side borders.)

Join border to top of quilt. Repeat to make and join bottom border.

4. To make 1 side border, fold 1 remaining border strip in half; mark to find center. From center line, mark fencepost locations every 10½". At each end of border, you will have 1 short section with a length of 5¾".

❖ QUILT SMART ❖

Cutting the Pieces

To make cutting easier, we've given measurements instead of templates for most of the pieces in Rita's quilt. If you prefer to cut your pieces using templates, use these measurements to make your own templates to speed you on your way.

For each block, you will need one fat quarter (or ⅜ yard) of one print for the sky, plus seven or eight print scraps for the barn, silo, and windmill. For each sky, barn, etc., cut all listed pieces from a single print. After you cut all pieces for a block, pin them together or place in a zip-top plastic bag to keep them organized.

For the sky:
1 (3½" x 21½") strip
1 (3½" x 15½") strip
6 A (3½" square)
4 B*

2 C (2" square)
4 D (2" x 3½")
1 E**
1 E rev.***
2 F (use template)

For the barnyard:
1 (3½" x 21½") rectangle

For the barn:
1 A (3½" square)
2 C (2" square)
7 D (2" x 3½")

For the roof:
1 A (3½" square)
1 B*
2 D (2" x 3½")
2 E**

For the chimney:
1 D (2" x 3½")
1 E rev.***

For the roof gable:
2 A (3½" square)
2 E**

2 E rev.***

For the barn door:
2 D (2" x 3½")

For the barn windows:
2 C (2" square)

For the silo:
4 A (3½" square)
1 B*
1 C (2" square)
1 D (2" x 3½")
1 E **
2 G (use template)

For the windmill:
4 B*
4 (1" x 6") strips

*For 2 Bs, cut 1 (2⅜") square; cut in half diagonally.
**For 2 Es, cut 1 (3¾" x 2¼") rectangle; cut in half diagonally from lower left to upper right.
***For 2 Es rev., cut 1 (3¾" x 2¼") rectangle; cut in half diagonally from upper left to lower right.

From white bias, cut 20 (12"-long) strips, 4 (8½"-long) strips, and 13 (5¾"-long) strips. Appliqué 12"-long bias strips in crisscross fashion to make 10 fence sections. At each end of border, appliqué 2 (8½"-long) strips to make 1 short fence section. Appliqué 11 (5¾"-long) strips to make fenceposts.

Join border to 1 side of quilt, butting corners. Appliqué remaining 5¾"-long bias strips to top and bottom borders, completing fence and covering seams.

5. Repeat Step 4 to make and join second side border.

Quilting

Quilt in-the-ditch around each block and around barns, windmills, and silos. Quilt 1½"

crosshatch pattern across silo. For sky, quilt clouds, sun rays, or rain, as shown in photograph; or quilt as desired.

Finished Edges

Bind with straight-grain or bias binding made from white.

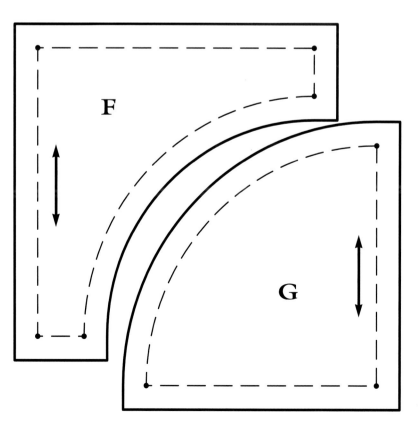

Lou Beasley
Centralia, Missouri

*A*lthough Lou Beasley began taking quilting classes 14 years ago, her interest in quilts actually started much earlier. "My mother quilted when I was young, and sometimes I would attend a quilt gathering with her," Lou says. "The ladies would give me small pieces of material to sew to keep me busy."

"I really enjoy quilting the piece because that's what can make or break the picture."

During those quilt gatherings, Lou's mother and great-grandmother taught her the importance of quality handwork. Now she studies antique quilts to learn how to fine-tune her skills.

"Antique quilts can teach us a lot about quilting, piecing, and appliqué," she says. Antique quilts are also a great source of design inspiration. "For reference, I will sometimes take pictures of them at estate sales and auctions," she says.

Most evenings you can find Lou nestled in her favorite chair in the living room quilting in front of her family. "I like to be with them," she says, "and I find that they appreciate my quilting much more because they can relate to the time and effort it takes to make a quilt."

Charade
1995

Lou named her quilt *Charade* because it seemed to be such a puzzle. "It always presented a question of what I should do next," she says. "I knew I wanted a border area where I could do some special quilting, but in order for this piece to look complete, I felt it needed pieced borders as well."

Charade is an original design that Lou hand-pieced and hand-quilted. She chose to make it from scraps of 1930s reproduction fabrics because the fabrics reminded her of the soft quilts she grew up with. She also chose to use a cotton batting to give it the additional feel of a soft, antique quilt.

Charade

Finished Quilt Size
82½" x 94½"

Number of Blocks and Finished Size
184 blocks   4½" x 4½"

Fabric Requirements
White	3¾ yards
Green	3¾ yards
Pastel prints	2¾ yards total
Pastel solids	1½ yards total
Backing	5¾ yards
Green for binding	¾ yard

Pieces to Cut
White
  2 (5" x 50") border strips
  2 (5" x 71") border strips
  736 (2"-square) A*
  104 D
Green
  2 (2" x 47") inner border strips
  2 (2" x 62") inner border strips
  2 (2" x 59") outer border strips
  2 (2" x 74") outer border strips
  596 C
Pastel prints
  920 (2"-square) A**
Pastel solids
  492 B

*If quick-piecing, cut 36 (2"-wide) crosswise strips (selvage to selvage) instead of 736 As.
**If quick-piecing, cut 44 (2"-wide) crosswise strips instead of 920 As.

Quilt Top Assembly

1. To make 1 nine-patch block, join 4 white As and 5 As

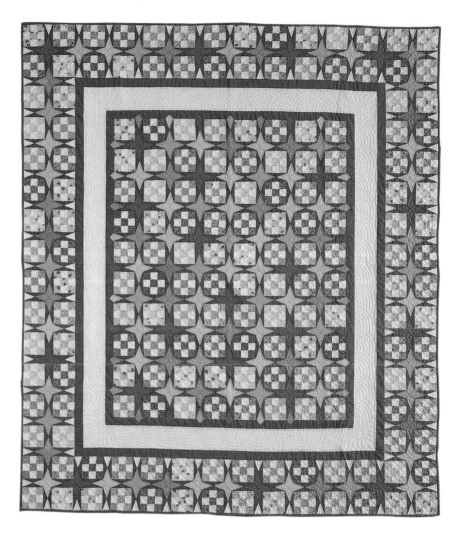

of the same pastel print, as shown in photograph. (For quick-piecing instructions, see *Quilt Smart* on page 87.) Repeat to make 184 nine-patch blocks.

2. To make 1 inner sashing block, join 2 green Cs and 2 Bs of different pastel solids as shown in *Inner Sashing Block Assembly Diagram*. Repeat to

Inner Sashing Block Assembly Diagram

make 194 inner sashing blocks.

3. To make 1 outer sashing block, join 1 B, 2 Cs, and 1 D as shown in *Outer Sashing Block Assembly Diagram*. Repeat to

Outer Sashing Block Assembly Diagram

make 104 outer sashing blocks.

4. To make center of quilt, arrange 80 nine-patch blocks and 142 inner sashing blocks on floor or design wall, matching colors of adjacent Bs to make stars as shown in photograph.

5. When satisfied with arrangement, join nine-patch blocks and inner sashing blocks in 10 horizontal rows. Join rows alternately with inner sashing blocks.

6. To join green inner top border, align raw edges of quilt top and 1 (2" x 47") border strip, right sides facing, with quilt top uppermost. Stitch from edge of quilt to seam line of first B; backstitch. Skipping to opposite seam line of first B, backstitch to lock seam and stitch to seam line of second B *(Figure 1)*. Continue stitching across nine-patch blocks, skip-

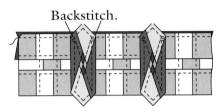

Backstitch.

Figure 1

ping Bs, to end of border.

Press border away from quilt. Turn quilt to right side. Appliqué points of Bs to border.

7. Repeat Step 6 for bottom border.

8. In same manner, join 2" x 62" border strips to sides of quilt, butting corners.

9. Join 5" x 50" white borders to top and bottom of quilt. Join 5" x 71" white borders to sides of quilt, butting corners.

10. Join 2" x 59" green border strips to top and bottom of quilt. Join 2" x 74" green border strips to sides of quilt, butting corners.

11. To make top pieced border, arrange 2 rows of 10 nine-patch blocks and 11 outer sashing blocks. Between rows, arrange 10 inner sashing blocks, matching colors of adjacent Bs to make stars as shown in photograph. When satisfied with arrangement, join blocks. Join to top of quilt.

12. Repeat Step 11 to make and join bottom pieced border.

13. To make 1 side pieced border, arrange 2 rows of 16 nine-patch blocks and 15 outer sashing blocks. Between rows, arrange 16 inner sashing blocks as in Step 11. Join blocks. Join to side of quilt.

14. Repeat Step 13 to make and join second side pieced border.

Quilting

Quilt ¼" inside all B and D pieces. Quilt an "X" across each A. Quilt fan pattern in white borders, or quilt as desired.

Finished Edges

Bind with straight-grain or bias binding made from green.

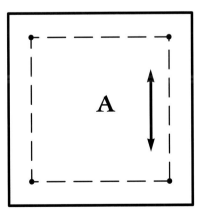

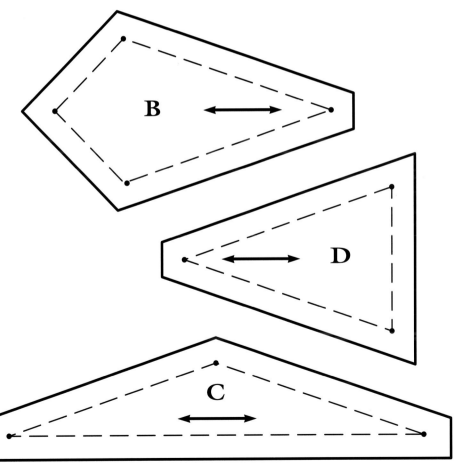

Peg Voll
Clinton, Michigan

*S*ometimes burnout can be a positive thing. For Peg Voll, tiring of crafts opened the world of quilting to her.

"I'm in the process of making quilts for my kids as they marry—one down, one going down, two to go!"

"I saw a quilting magazine, bought it, and then taught myself how to piece and quilt," Peg says.

Perhaps Peg is still having fun with her quilting because she gets such pleasure from each step of the process. "I enjoy all the steps," she says. "That's why I have so many quilts in stages."

Although she recently went back to work full time, Peg still manages to devote some time each day to quilting. "I'm just working a little slower," she says. "But I'm still quilting and still having fun!"

The Cow Quilt
1994

When Peg decided that she wanted to make a black and white quilt, she had no idea how many challenges lay ahead! To begin with, this was Peg's first original design; she had never made a quilt without a pattern before.

Naturally, she was a little nervous. Then she had trouble finding someone who could draw a cow for her. "Boy, did I get some strange-looking cows," says Peg. Finally her friend Sue Willis drew just the cow Peg wanted for her quilt. But her difficulties weren't over quite yet.

"Once I started to hand-quilt it, I decided I would never again use so much black," she says. "I couldn't see the needle go in or out of the fabric. I had to do all the quilting on the black areas in the bright sunlight! It was definitely an experience!"

In the end, though, Peg decided that *The Cow Quilt* was well worth all the trouble. It won both a blue ribbon and Best of Show in the 1996 Lenawec County Fair.

The Cow Quilt

Finished Quilt Size
86½" x 116½"

Number of Blocks and Finished Size

6 blocks   24" x 24"

Fabric Requirements

White	6 yards
Black solid	2½ yards
Large black print	3¼ yards
Small black print	2¼ yards
Backing	8 yards*

*Or 3½ yards of 108"-wide backing fabric.

Pieces to Cut

White
- 2 (21½" x 80") panels
- 3 A
- 3 (12½"-square) B
- 48 C**
- 12 (6½"-square) D
- 6 E
- 6 I
- 44 (2") squares for border
- 74 (5") squares***

Black
- 4 (1¼" x 78½") border strips
- 2 (1¼" x 59") border strips
- 3 (12½"-square) B
- 48 C**

Large black print
- 2 (4" x 101") border strips
- 2 (8½" x 87") border strips
- 3 A
- 6 F
- 6 G
- 6 H
- 6 J
- 6 K
- 6 L
- 6 M
- 6 N
- 6 O

- 6 P
- 46 (2") squares for border
- 38 (5") squares***

Small black print
- 3 (2" x 75½") sashing strips
- 2 (2" x 50") sashing strips
- 4 (2" x 24½") sashing strips
- 36 (5" squares)***

**Cut 24 (6⅞") squares; cut each in half diagonally for 48 Cs.
***For prairie points.

Quilt Top Assembly

1. To make 1 black star block, fold 1 white B in half horizontally and vertically. Finger-press to mark center. Unfold. Appliqué 1 large black print A to center of square.

Referring to *Block Assembly Diagram*, join appliquéd B, 8 white Cs, 8 black Cs, and 4 white Ds as shown to complete 1 block. Repeat to make 3 black star blocks.

2. To make 1 white star block, mark center of 1 black B as described. Appliqué 1 white A to center of square. Join B, 8 white Cs, 8 black Cs, and 4 black Ds as in Step 1. Repeat to make 3 white star blocks.

3. To make top row, join 2 white star blocks, 1 black star block, and 2 (2" x 24½") small black print sashing strips as

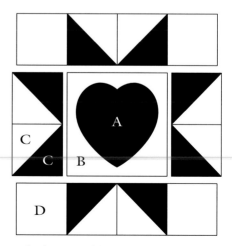

Block Assembly Diagram

shown in *Quilt Top Assembly Diagram*. Join 1 (2" x 75½") small black print sashing strip to top and bottom edges of row.

4. To make bottom row, join 2 black star blocks, 1 white star block, and 2 (2" x 24½") small black print sashing strips as shown in *Quilt Top Assembly Diagram*. Join remaining 2" x 75½" small black print sashing strip to bottom of row.

5. Join rows.

6. For 1 side sashing strip, join 1 (2") large black print square to each end of 1 (2" x 50") small black print strip. Join to 1 side of top, butting corners. Repeat for second side sashing strip.

7. To make top pieced border, join 22 (2") white squares alternately with 21 (2") large black print squares. Join 1 (1¼" x 78½") black strip to top and bottom edges of pieced strip. Join to top of quilt. Repeat for bottom border.

8. Join 1¼" x 59" black strips to sides of quilt, butting corners.

9. To make 1 appliquéd panel, fold 1 (21½" x 80") white strip in half vertically; finger-press to mark center. Fold in half again; finger-press. Unfold strip. Referring to *Appliqué Placement Diagram* for arrangement, center 1 each of pieces E–O on 1 creased mark. Pin pieces in place. Appliqué to strip to make 1 cow. Repeat to make 3 cows on panel, as shown in photograph.

Repeat to make second appliquéd panel.

Appliqué Placement Diagram

10. Join panels to top and bottom of quilt.

11. Join 4" x 101" large black print border strips to sides of quilt. Join 8½" x 87" large black print border strips to top and bottom of quilt, butting corners.

Quilt Top Assembly Diagram

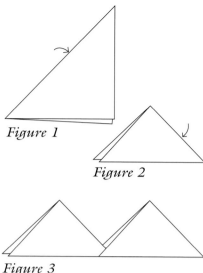

Figure 1

Figure 2

Figure 3

Prairie Point Diagram

12. To make 1 side prairie point border, fold the following 5" squares as shown in *Prairie Point Diagram:* 21 white, 11 large black print, and 11 small black print. Referring to photograph for color placement, pin prairie points to 1 side of quilt top, aligning raw edges and overlapping points as required to fit edge of quilt. Baste. Repeat for opposite side.

13. In same manner, fold, pin, and baste 16 white squares, 8 large black print squares, and 7 small black print squares for top border. Repeat for bottom border.

Quilting

Quilt in-the-ditch around all cow pieces, sashing strips, and border strips. Quilt ¼" inside seam lines on star blocks. Quilt background of appliquéd panels with 1½" crosshatch pattern. Quilt star blocks and borders as desired.

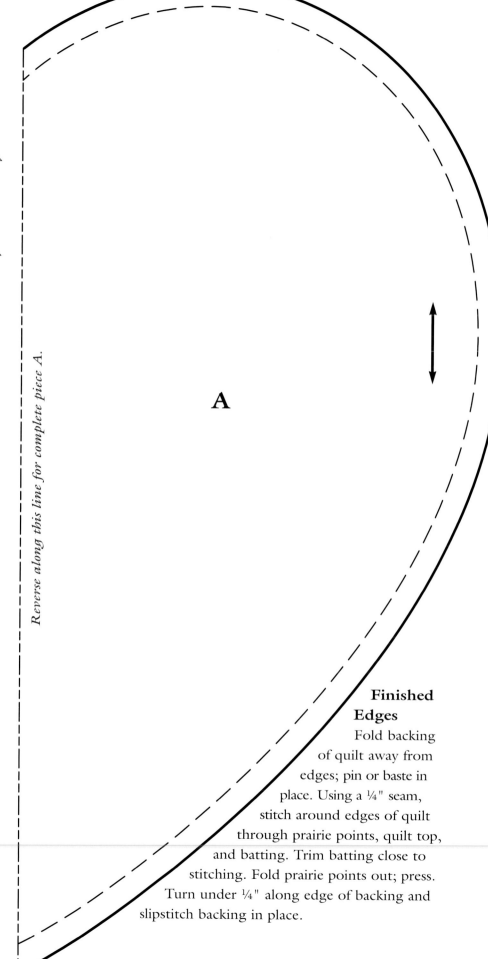

Reverse along this line for complete piece A.

A

Finished Edges

Fold backing of quilt away from edges; pin or baste in place. Using a ¼" seam, stitch around edges of quilt through prairie points, quilt top, and batting. Trim batting close to stitching. Fold prairie points out; press. Turn under ¼" along edge of backing and slipstitch backing in place.

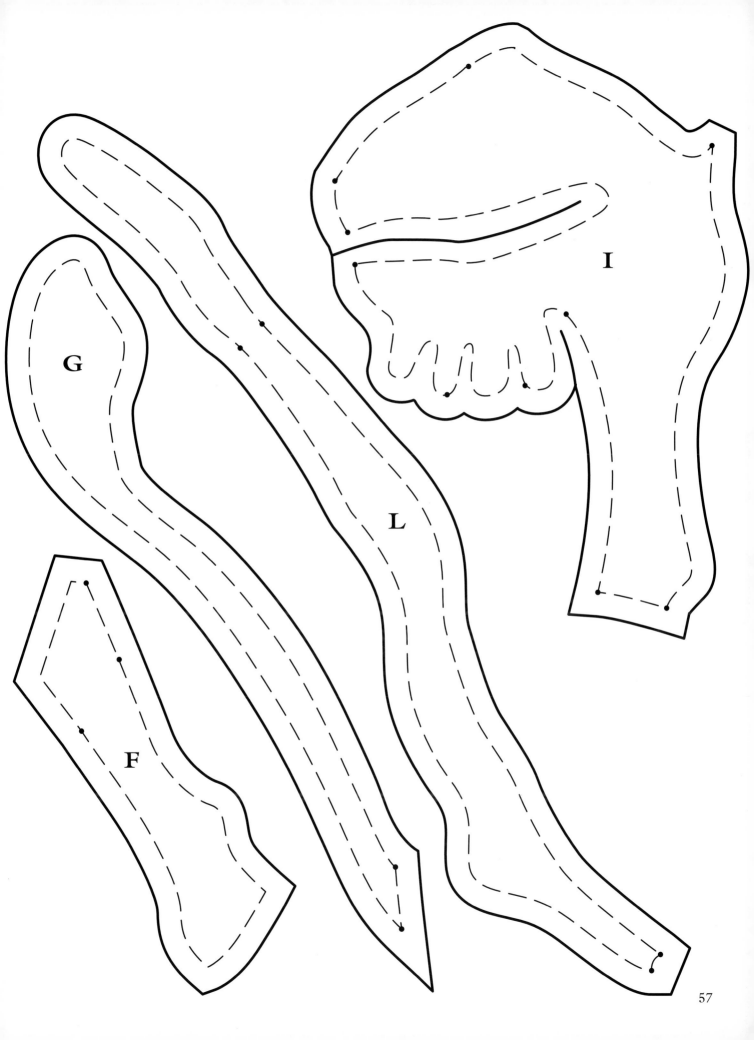

I

G

L

F

57

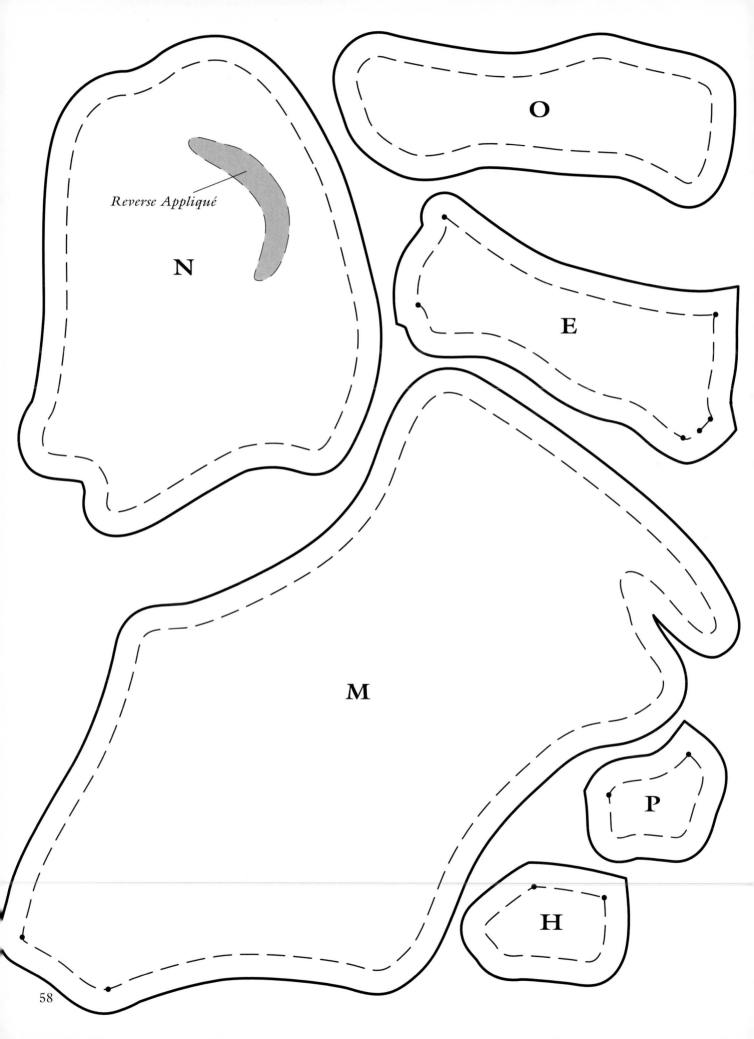

Reverse Appliqué

N

O

E

M

P

H

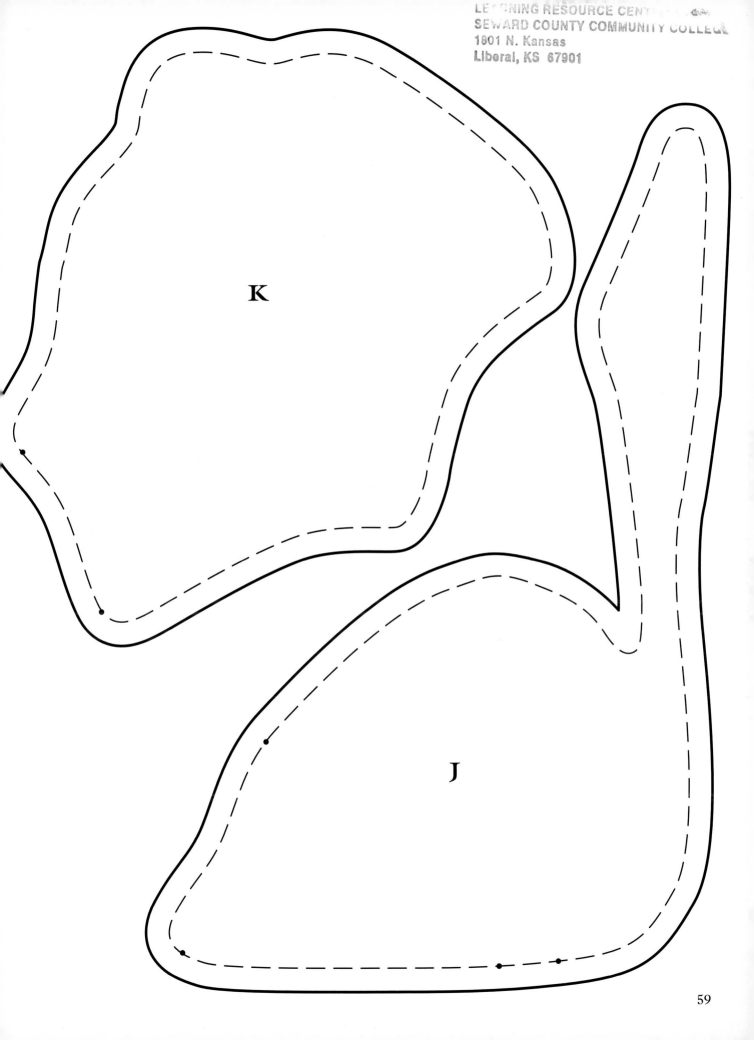

K

J

Darlene Christopherson
China Spring, Texas

South Dakota native Darlene Christopherson fell in love with antique quilts when she lived in northern Virginia in the late 1970s.

"We were close to everything there," she remembers. "the DAR Museum in Washington, the album quilts in Baltimore. I fell in love with the intricate appliqué and decided to learn how to do that."

So she signed up for a number of classes at quilt shops near her home. "My husband works for the government," she says, "and I was convinced that we were going to move every year or two. I was worried about the lack of shops in other parts of the country, so I decided to take all the classes there were before we had to leave Virginia!"

During this marathon class-taking session, Darlene met and became friends with Jinny Beyer. "Jinny became interested in my work, and I spent several years on the staff at her annual Hilton Head Island retreat," she says. "Then, after we moved back to South Dakota, I began traveling to teach, and I've been doing it ever since."

Peacock Medallion
1996

Darlene's design for *Peacock Medallion* had its beginnings in the antique Baltimore Album quilts and classes of her days in Virginia.

"Jinny Beyer taught a class on medallion quilts that I took," she says. "But I didn't want to do the Mariner's Compass medallion that the other students were doing. I wanted something different."

In one of the museum exhibitions, Darlene had seen and sketched a picture of an unusual quilt from the 1800s: a quilt with a painted central medallion of peacocks. "I simplified it quite a lot," she says. She completed the appliqué in about a year, taking time to plan each border as she added it. "I'd pin it up on the wall and think about it," she says. "Then when I finished that one, I'd pin it up and think about the next one."

Then came the move to South Dakota. Darlene knew her sewing equipment and materials would be packed up for quite a while after they moved, so she made sure that the *Peacock Medallion* and her quilting hoop were close to the top. "I had it basted and ready to go before we moved," she says. "Then I left everything else in the boxes and just pulled out this one project."

61

Peacock Medallion

Finished Quilt Size
72½" x 72½"

Fabric Requirements

Ivory solid	1¼ yards
Ivory print	2 yards
Blue stripe for borders	3 yards*
Dark blue print	⅛ yard
Light blue print	⅛ yard
Medium brown print	¾ yard
Dark brown print	⅛ yard
Green prints	1 yard total
Red prints	1¼ yards total
Purple prints	½ yard total
Backing	4½ yards

*Includes fabric for binding.

Other Materials
Green embroidery floss

Pieces to Cut

Ivory solid
- 2 (13⅝") squares
- 4 (6½" x 32½") border panels
- 1 (14¾") square

Ivory print
- 1 (18½") square
- 2 (12⅞") squares
- 8 (7¼" x 33¼") border panels

Blue stripe for borders
- 4 (3¾" x 33¼") strips
- 4 (3¾" x 51¾") strips
- 4 (4¾" x 73") strips

Dark blue print
- 1 B
- 1 B rev.

Darlene cut several butterflies from a printed fabric and appliquéd them randomly to her quilt.

Light blue print
- 1 A
- 1 A rev.

Medium brown print
- 1 E
- 1 E rev.
- 1 G

Dark brown print
- 1 D
- 1 D rev.
- 54 Y
- 22 Y rev.

Green prints
- 105 H
- 78 I

Red prints
- 1 C
- 1 C rev.
- 16 F
- 41 J
- 1 J rev.
- 1 K

- 1 K rev.
- 74 L
- 37 M
- 33 M rev.
- 1 N
- 1 N rev.
- 1 O
- 1 O rev.
- 44 P
- 8 Q
- 16 R
- 16 S
- 48 T
- 44 U
- 16 V
- 4 V rev.
- 12 W
- 1 X
- 1 X rev.

Purple prints
- 380 Z

Quilt Top Assembly

1. From remaining medium brown print, make 300" of 1"-wide bias. From remaining green prints, make 50" of 1"-wide bias. Press under ¼" on each long edge. Set aside.

2. To make central medallion, cut each 13⅝" ivory solid square in half diagonally to make 4 corner triangles. Join 1 triangle to each corner of 18½" ivory print square.

Referring to *Central Medallion Appliqué Placement Diagram* and *Inner Corner Appliqué Placement Diagram* on pages 64 and 65, appliqué pieces to medallion and triangles as shown. Using 2 strands of embroidery floss, outline-stitch grapevine tendrils as shown.

Join 3¾" x 33¼" blue stripe borders to edges of medallion, mitering corners.

3. To make inner appliquéd border, join 6½" x 32½" ivory solid border panels to edges of quilt. Cut each 12⅞" ivory print square in half diagonally to make 4 corner triangles. Join to corners of quilt as shown in *Quilt Top Assembly Diagram,* trimming border panels as required.

Referring to *Inner Border Appliqué Placement Diagram* on page 65, appliqué pieces to border panels and triangles as shown. Using 2 strands of embroidery floss, outline-stitch grapevine tendrils as shown.

Join 3¾" x 51¾" blue stripe borders to edges of quilt, mitering corners.

4. To make outer appliquéd border, cut 14¾" ivory solid triangle into quarters diagonally to make 4 side triangles. Join 1 triangle to 2 (7¼" x 33¼") ivory print border panels as shown in *Quilt Top Assembly Diagram,* trimming panels as required.

Referring to *Outer Border Appliqué Placement Diagram,* on page 65, appliqué pieces to borders as shown. Using 2 strands of embroidery floss, outline-stitch grapevine tendrils as shown.

Join 4¾" x 73" blue stripe borders to edges of quilt, mitering corners.

Quilting

Quilt in-the-ditch around all appliquéd pieces. Quilt borders with feather plumes and 1" cross-hatching as shown in photograph, or quilt as desired.

Finished Edges

Bind with straight-grain or bias binding made from blue stripe.

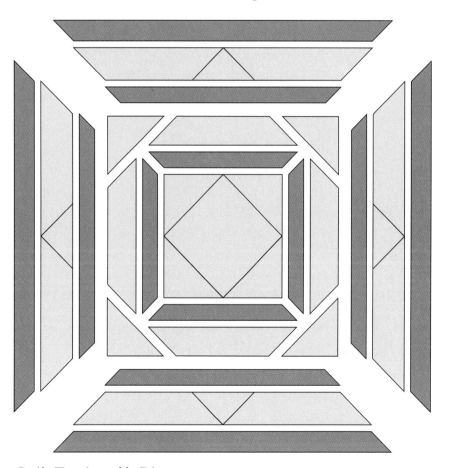

Quilt Top Assembly Diagram

Central Medallion Appliqué Placement Diagram

Inner Border Appliqué Placement Diagram

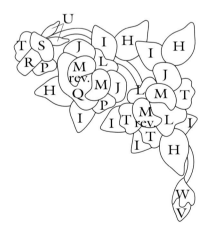

Inner Corner Appliqué Placement Diagram

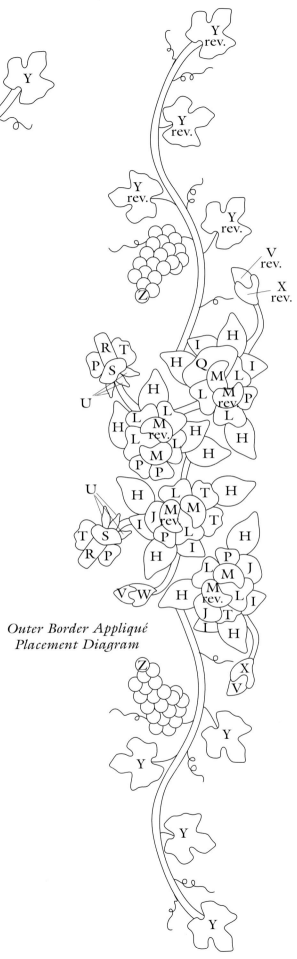

*Outer Border Appliqué
Placement Diagram*

65

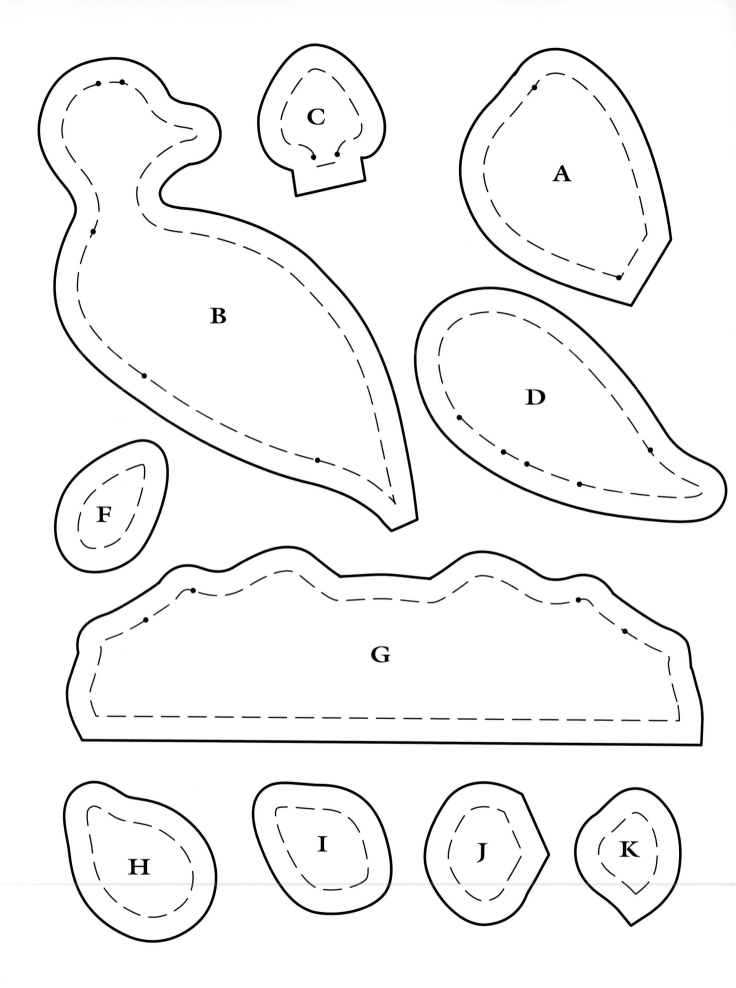

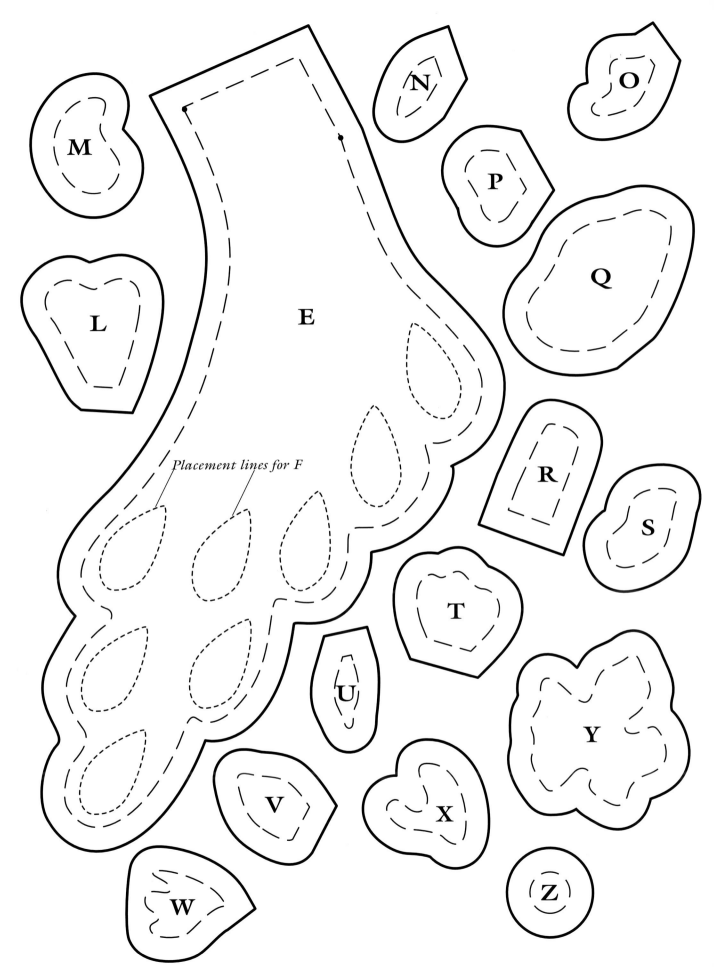

Placement lines for F

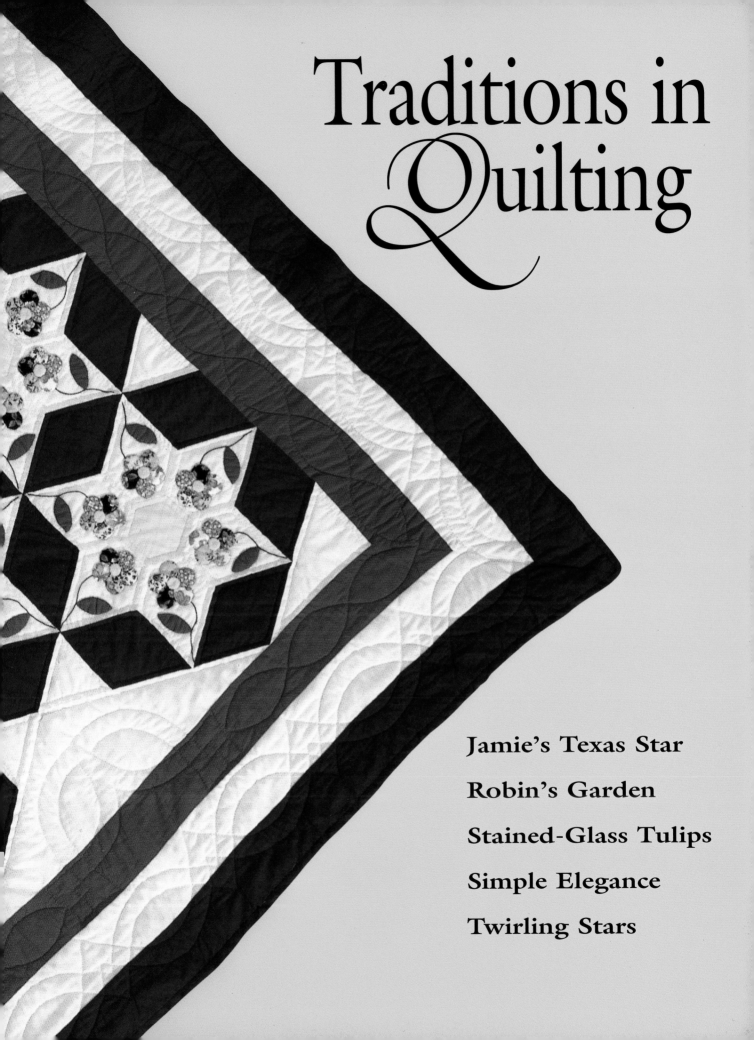

Traditions in Quilting

Jamie's Texas Star

Robin's Garden

Stained-Glass Tulips

Simple Elegance

Twirling Stars

Margaret Gulledge
Odenville, Alabama

Close friends often give us wonderful gifts. For Margaret Gulledge, one of the best gifts she ever received was from her friend Coleen Rikard. It was Coleen who helped Margaret get started quilting, and the two have been quilting together ever since. Margaret made her first quilt in 1986. "After that I was hooked," she says. "I started collecting scraps, and buying quilt material became an addiction."

Margaret quilts primarily for her family and friends, and she is currently making a quilt for each of her eight grandchildren. "The first quilt for a grandchild was a star quilt I made for my oldest granddaughter, Melissa," she says. "I made it from scraps from dresses I had made for my granddaughters. Next came a *Dresden Plate* for Ashley, *Schoolhouses* for Sumer, and then *Jamie's Texas Star*. And I still have four grandsons to go!"

Jamie's Texas Star
1996

When it came time for Margaret's granddaughter Jamie to choose the pattern she wanted, she first chose a postage stamp pattern made entirely of 1" squares.

"I thought if she could look at other patterns, she would choose an easier one!" says Margaret wryly. Jamie's next choice, from which she would not waver despite repeated encouragement to look at others, was the appliquéd star pattern that eventually became *Jamie's Texas Star*.

Jamie obviously loves quilts with lots of small pieces! The flowers alone required almost a thousand 1"-diameter circles to make the flower petals, and 200 even smaller circles to form the centers!

Quilt Top Assembly

1. Appliqué 5 pastel print Gs, 1 H, and 1 I to 1 A as shown on pattern piece. Using 2 strands of floss, outline-stitch flower stem and leaf vein. Repeat to appliqué 6 As.

Referring to *Star Assembly Diagram*, join 6 appliquéd As and 1 B as shown to complete 1 star. Repeat to make 32 stars.

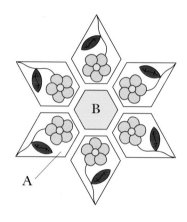

Star Assembly Diagram

Jamie's Texas Star

Finished Quilt Size
82" x 97"

Fabric Requirements
White	5 yards
Blue	3¼ yards*
Green	2¼ yards
Yellow	1 yard
Pastel prints	2½ yards total
Backing	5¼ yards

*Includes fabric for binding.

Other Materials
Green embroidery floss

Pieces to Cut
White
  2 (3½" x 91⅜") border strips
  2 (3½" x 76½") border strips
  6 (6" x 23½") rectangles**
  192 A
  20 D
Blue
  2 (3½" x 97⅜") border strips
  2 (3½" x 82½") border strips
  119 C
Green
  2 (3½" x 70½") border strips
  2 (3½" x 85⅜") border strips
  192 I
Yellow
  32 B
  192 H
Pastel prints
  960 G***

**See Step 2.
***Cut 192 G from each print.

2. Fold 1 (6" x 23½") white rectangle in half vertically, as shown in *Cutting Diagram for E and F*. Using measurements shown in diagram, cut 1 (6" x 23½") triangle for E on folded edge. Cut 2 (8½" x 4¼") triangles for F from remaining fabric.

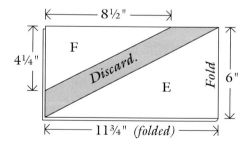

Cutting Diagram for E and F

3. Join stars with Cs, Ds, Es, and Fs as shown on *Quilt Top Assembly Diagram*.

4. Join 3½" x 70½" green border strips to top and bottom of quilt. Join 3½" x 85⅜" green border strips to sides of quilt, mitering corners.

5. Join 3½" x 91⅜" white border strips to sides of quilt. Join 3½" x 76½" white border strips to top and bottom of quilt, mitering corners.

6. Join 3½" x 97⅜" blue border strips to sides of quilt. Join 3½" x 82½" blue border strips to top and bottom of quilt, mitering corners.

Quilting

Quilt in-the-ditch around all pieces and borders. Quilt borders and side triangles E and F as desired.

Finished Edges

Bind with straight-grain or bias binding made from blue.

Quilt Top Assembly Diagram

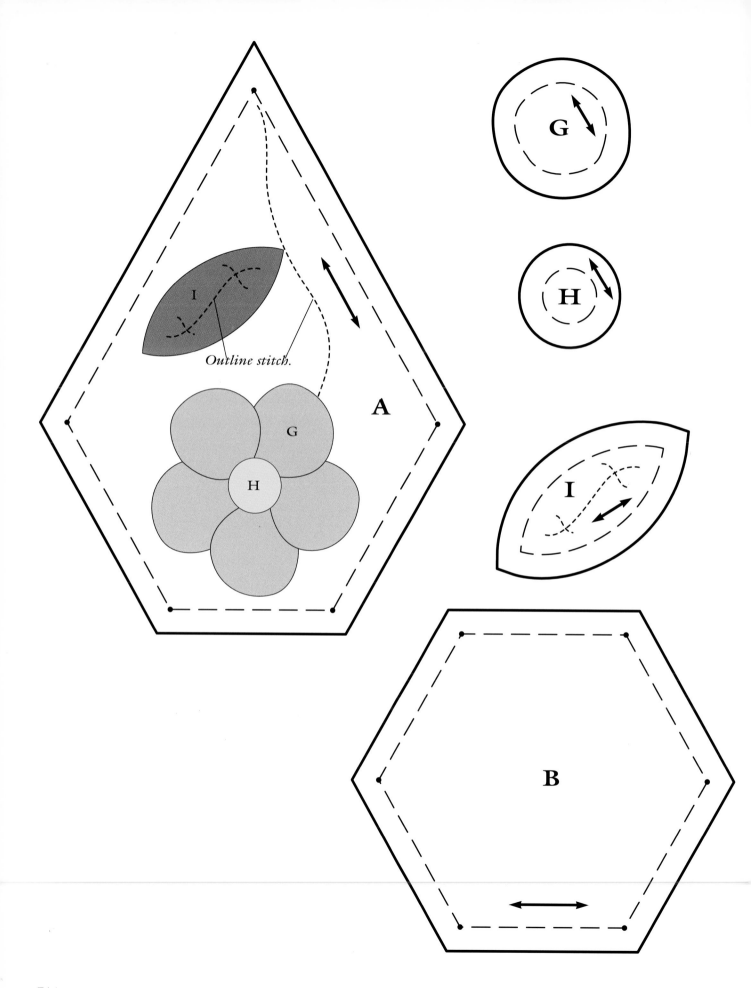

Outline stitch.

A

G

H

I

B

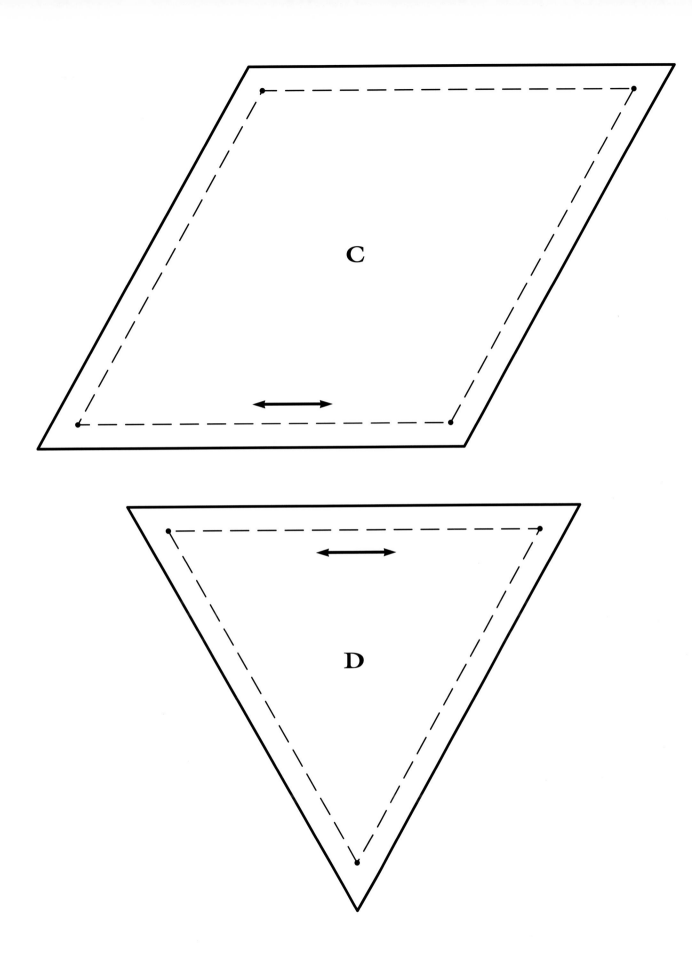

C

D

Barbara Hollinger
Edina, Minnesota

Retired materials engineer Barbara Hollinger was lured into quilting just after college by her love of color and sewing. "I didn't do too much at first," she says, "just a few samplers. I just didn't like the fabrics that were available then." But after working for several years and retiring to raise her children, Barb discovered an entirely new world of fabric choices and a quilting community exploding with ideas.

"Although my quilts are evolving from traditional, I like the play of patterns and the rhythm of repeated designs within traditional quilt patterns."

"I'm mostly self-taught," she says, "but I've had a few technique and design classes to spur me on. Once I learned machine quilting from Harriet Hargrave, there was no stopping me! I love hand quilting and appliqué, but most of my work is done by machine. Too many ideas and not enough time!"

Robin's Garden
1995

"I usually start a quilt with a traditional design and then jazz it up," Barbara says.

At the time she began *Robin's Garden,* Barbara had just completed a quilt made from Depression-era Dresden Plate blocks. For several years, she had been collecting yellow prints to make a sunny quilt for her daughter Robin's sixth birthday. And the Dresden Plate block, redrafted and embellished, provided just the showcase for those prints.

"We've moved four times in eight years," Barbara says, "and it took three of those four moves to finish Robin's quilt. With each move, I made it a goal to get unpacked and organized enough to get it back out and get to work again. It meant the new house was really home."

Robin's Garden

Finished Quilt Size
87" x 87"

Number of Blocks and Finished Size
9 blocks   14" x 14"

Fabric Requirements
Lavender	7½ yards
Purple	¾ yard
Floral	1½ yards
Gold	¾ yard
Green	¾ yard
Yellow prints	4½ yards total
Backing	8 yards*
Lavender for binding	¾ yard

*Or 2¾ yards of 90"-wide fabric.

Pieces to Cut
Lavender
    8 (16½" x 44") outer border strips
    9 (14½") squares
Purple
    2 (22⅛") squares**
Floral
    4 (1¼" x 45") inner border strips
    8 (1¼" x 23") middle border strips
Gold
    4 (1" x 45") inner border strips
    8 (1" x 23") middle border strips
Yellow prints
    88 A
    252 B

**Cut each square in half diagonally for 4 corner triangles.

Quilt Top Assembly

1. To make 1 block, join 4 As and 12 Bs along long edges to make 1 pieced circle. Fold 1 lavender square into quarters diagonally; finger-press. Unfold. Referring to *Block Assembly Diagram*, appliqué pieced circle to block with points of As toward corners of square as shown. Appliqué 1 C over center

of circle, covering raw edges. Repeat to make 9 blocks.

2. Join blocks in 3 rows of 3 as shown in *Quilt Top Assembly Diagram.* Join rows.

3. To make inner border, join 1 (45"-long) gold inner border strip and 1 (45"-long) floral inner border strip along long edges. Repeat to make 4 borders. Join to edges of quilt with gold strip innermost, mitering corners.

4. To make middle border, join 1 (23"-long) gold strip to 1 (23"-long) floral strip along long edges. Repeat to make 8 borders.

5. Referring to *Quilt Top Assembly Diagram,* join 1 middle border to each side of 1 corner triangle, gold strip innermost, mitering corners. Join 1

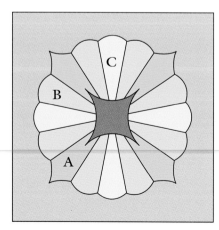

Block Assembly Diagram

(16½" x 44") lavender border to each side of triangle, mitering corners.

Repeat for remaining triangles.

6. Join corners to sides of quilt as shown in *Quilt Top Assembly Diagram.*

7. Referring to *Flower 1 Appliqué Placement Diagram,* join 3 As, 6 Bs, and 1 C as shown to make 1 Flower 1. Repeat to make 4 flowers.

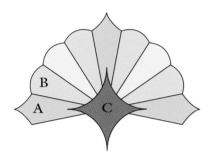

Flower 1 Appliqué Placement Diagram

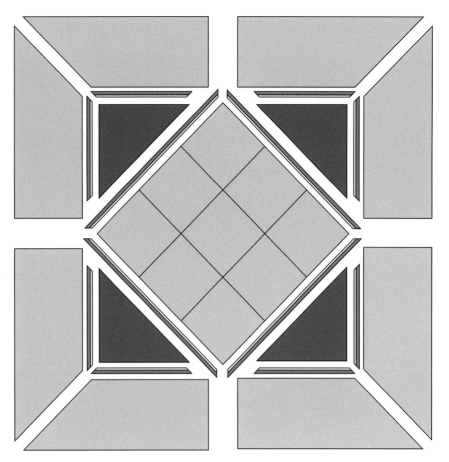

Quilt Top Assembly Diagram

8. Referring to *Flower 2 Appliqué Placement Diagram,* join 2 As, 3 Bs, and 1 D as shown to make 1 Flower 2. Repeat to make 20 flowers.

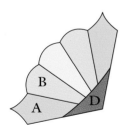

Flower 2 Appliqué Placement Diagram

9. Referring to *Flower 3 Appliqué Placement Diagram,* join 3 Bs and 1 E as shown to make 1 Flower 3. Repeat to make 20 flowers.

Flower 3 Appliqué Placement Diagram

10. From green, make 700" of ¾"-wide bias. Press under ¾" on each long side.

11. Referring to photograph for placement, appliqué bias to quilt to form vines.

12. Referring to photograph for placement, appliqué Flowers 1, 2, and 3 to quilt as shown.

Quilting

Outline-quilt around all appliqué pieces and border strips. Stipple-quilt background, or quilt as desired.

Finished Edges

Bind with straight-grain or bias binding made from lavender.

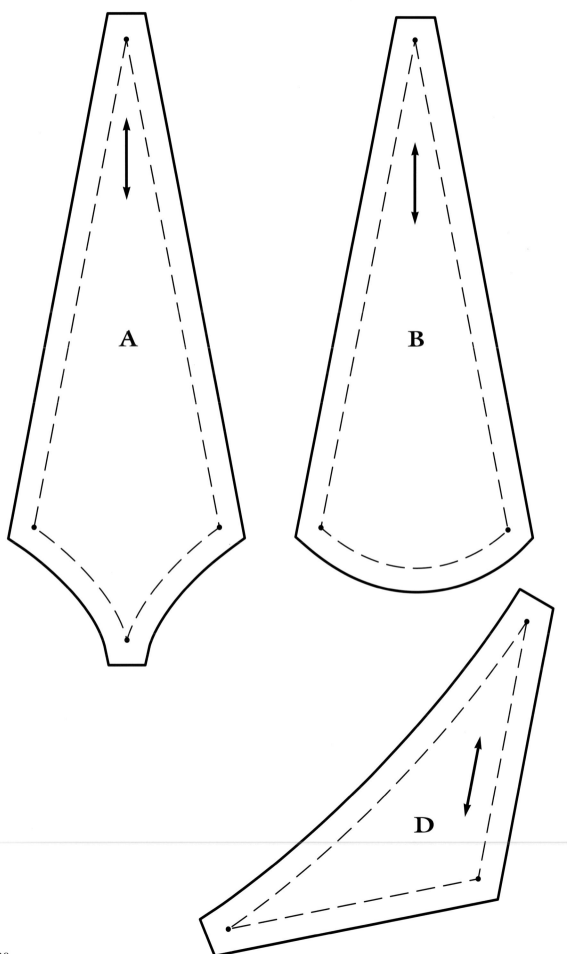

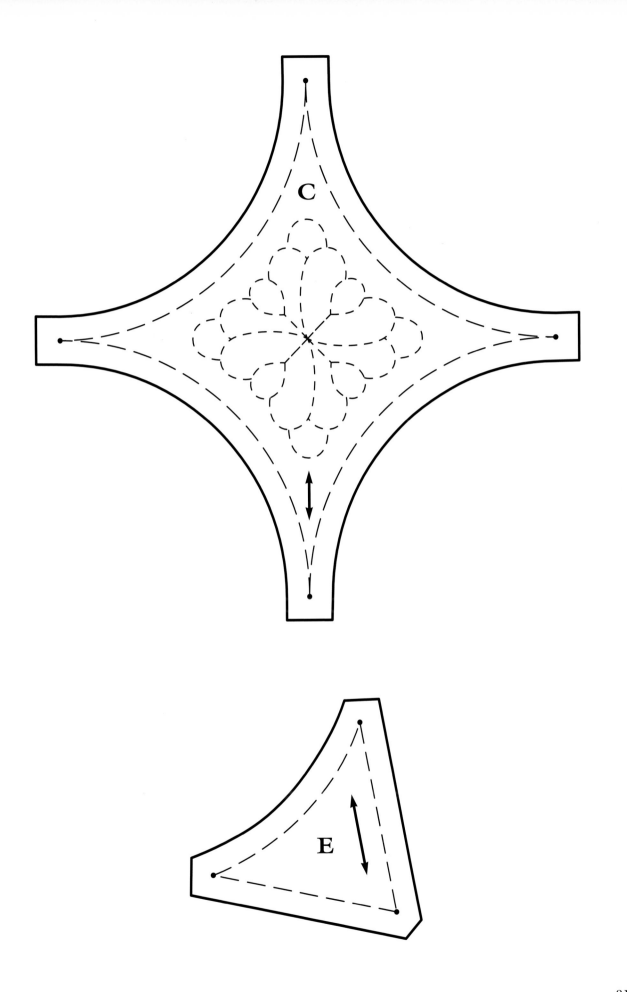

C

E

Hazel Keene Bryant
Blountsville, Alabama

"*M*y mother-in-law taught me to quilt after my second child was born," Hazel Bryant says. "I enjoyed having something to do, and I really needed the quilts!"

Once her children were grown, Hazel became involved with the local and county-level Homemakers Clubs. In 1988, she met Carol Reid of the Blount County Extension Service, who helped her and several others organize the Blount County Quilters' Guild, with Hazel as its first president.

"Quilting is a way of giving a bit of yourself to others. A lot of love goes into each quilt."

"Quilting has allowed me to make some wonderful friendships," Hazel says. "It's a way to help others and to pass on knowledge in the old way—person to person."

Stained-Glass Tulips
1992

Shortly after Hazel and Carol organized the Blount County Quilters' Guild, Carol suggested that Hazel teach a class in beginning quilting for some of the newer members. The Extension Service provided the pattern for *Stained-Glass Tulips,* originally designed by Sharon Heidingsfelder for the Arkansas Extension Service,

and Hazel jumped in with enthusiasm.

"The longer we worked on this project, the more the class members liked it," Hazel says. The top was finished during that class in 1988, but she didn't complete the hand quilting for several more years. The following year, it won Best of Show for the

State of Alabama at the Association for Family and Community Education Cultural Arts Show.

"Although I give away many of my quilts, I kept this one for myself, and it's still one of my favorites!" she says.

Stained-Glass Tulips
Finished Quilt Size
78" x 93"

Number of Blocks and Finished Size
9 blocks   14" x 19"

Fabric Requirements
Black	5 yards
White	1½ yards
Green	⅞ yard
Light pink	1 yard
Dark pink	1 yard
Backing	5½ yards
Black for binding	¾ yard

Pieces to Cut
Black*

    2 (12½" x 78½") border strips

    2 (12½" x 69½") border strips

    12 (3½" x 19½") sashing strips

    12 (3½" x 14½") sashing strips

    36 (1" x 15½") block border strips

    36 (1" x 14½") block border strips

White

    9 (10½" x 15½") rectangles

Green

    9 C

Light pink

    3 (1½"-wide) crosswise strips**

    10 (1½" x 15½") block border strips

    10 (1½" x 14½") block border strips

    9 B

Dark pink

    3 (1½"-wide) crosswise strips**

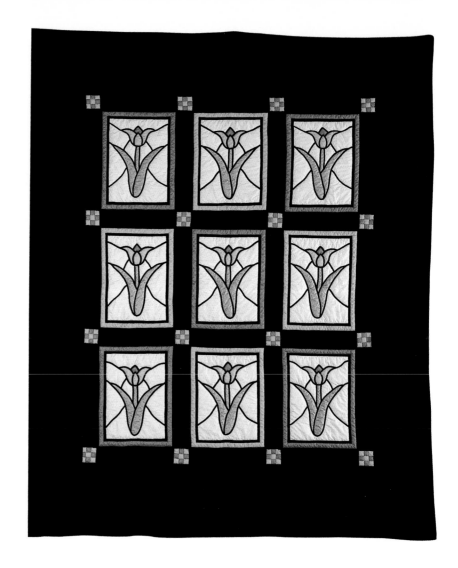

    8 (1½" x 15½") block border strips

    8 (1½" x 14½") block border strips

    9 A

*From remaining fabric, make 9 (1" x 1½") bias strips for appliqué.
**Cut strips selvage to selvage.

Quilt Top Assembly
1. Using full-size pattern on pages 86–87, transfer lines to 1 white rectangle.

2. Referring to *Appliqué Placement Diagram*, baste 1 A, 1 C, and 1 B to rectangle in that order.

3. Fold under ¼" on each long edge of 1 bias strip. Press. Referring to full-size pattern

and photograph, appliqué bias to block as shown, making sure raw ends are turned under or hidden.

4. Join 1 (1" x 15½") black strip to each long edge of 1 (1½" x 15½") dark pink strip. Join to 1 side of block. Repeat to make and join pieced strip to second side of block.

5. Join 1 (1" x 14½") black strip to each long edge of 1 (1½" x 14½") dark pink strip. Repeat. Join to top and bottom of block, mitering corners.

6. Repeat Steps 1–5 to make 5 blocks with dark pink pieced borders.

7. Repeat Steps 1–5 to make 4 blocks with light pink pieced borders.

8. Following instructions in *Quilt Smart* below, make 16 sashing blocks.

9. To make 1 sashing row, alternately join 4 sashing blocks and 3 (3½" x 14½") sashing strips as shown in *Quilt Top Assembly Diagram*. Repeat to make 4 sashing rows.

10. To make 1 block row, alternately join 3 blocks and 4 (3½" x 19½") sashing strips, alternating block colors as shown in *Quilt Top Assembly Diagram*. Repeat to make 3 block rows.

11. Join block rows alternately with sashing rows.

12. Join 12½" x 69½" black border strips to sides of quilt.

13. Join 12½" x 78½" black border strips to top and bottom of quilt, butting corners.

Quilting

Quilt in-the-ditch around all appliquéd pieces. Quilt borders and sashing strips as desired.

Finished Edges

Bind with straight-grain or bias binding made from black.

Quilt Top Assembly Diagram

❖ QUILT SMART ❖

Easy Nine-Patch Sashing Squares

1. Join 2 light pink strips and 1 dark pink strip along long edges as shown in *Figure A*. Using rotary cutter and ruler, cut 2 (1½"-wide) pieced units as shown.

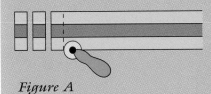

Figure A

2. Join remaining strips along long edges as shown in *Figure B*. Using rotary cutter

and ruler, cut 1 (1½"-wide) pieced unit as shown.

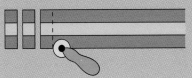

Figure B

3. Join pieced units as shown in *Figure C* to complete 1 nine-patch sashing square.

Figure C

4. Repeat to make 16 sashing squares.

Note: Add ⅛" seam allowance to pieces A, B, and C when making templates.

C

Placement lines for bias

Join at dashed line for complete pattern.

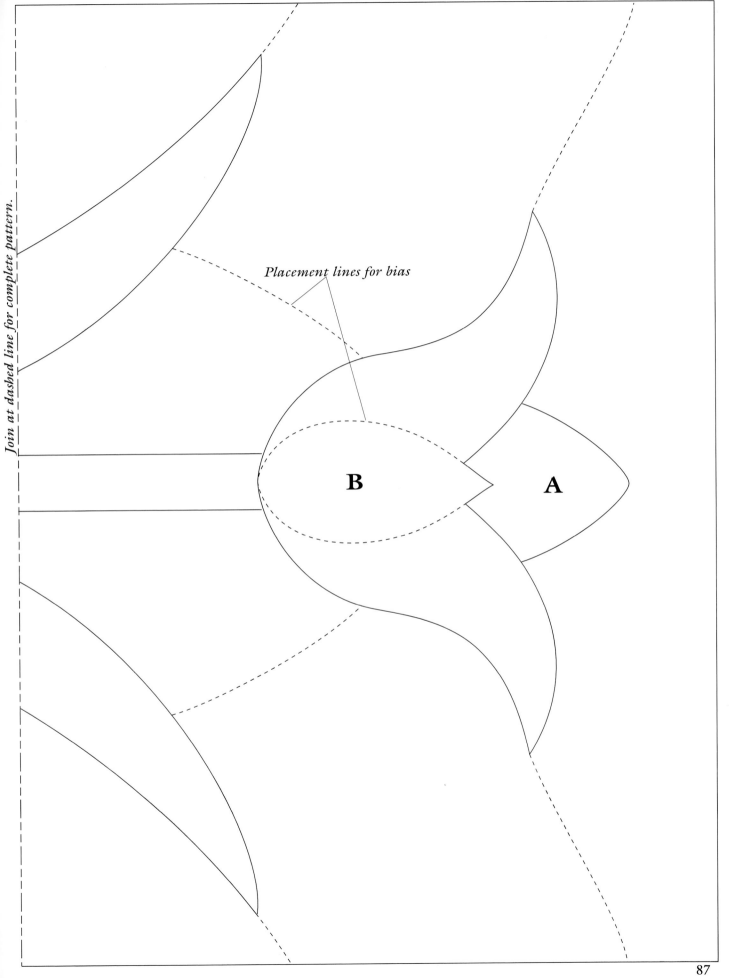

Join at dashed line for complete pattern.

Placement lines for bias

B

A

87

Jean Lohmar
Galesburg, Illinois

"*I*'ve always been interested in fabrics and sewing," says Jean Lohmar. "When my children were growing up, I worked on one quilt for several months each winter and then put it back in the drawer. That one intricately hand-appliquéd and hand-quilted piece

"My current challenges to myself are mock blindstitch appliqué and machine trapunto with wash-away thread."

took me almost 30 years to complete!" When the last of her seven children was in college, Jean fell in love with heirloom machine quilting. "I put my quilting thimble in the drawer and I haven't used it since!" she says.

Jean has won a number of awards for her extraordinary machine quilting, including Best of Show at the Illinois State Fair in 1996, and *two* Excellence for Machine Quilting awards from the National Quilting Association.

Simple Elegance
1995

"I fell in love with this pattern when I saw an antique Ohio Blue Leaf quilt in a magazine," Jean says. "Each year after the Christmas holidays, I begin designing a new quilt and always include a challenge to myself."

In January of 1995, Jean wanted to include mock blindstitch appliqué, trapunto, and intricate quilting—all by machine, of course. "I had also seen old quilts that contained piping with the binding," Jean says. "I thought the piping in the binding and border areas would add interest to this simple pattern."

Jean completed *Simple Elegance* in May of 1995— just five months after she set herself this challenge. Since then, the quilt has been exhibited at the American Quilters' Society show in Paducah, the National Quilting Association show, the Illinois State Fair, the Midwest Quilt Expo, and the Mississippi Valley Quilt Guild show.

Simple Elegance

Finished Quilt Size
84" x 99½"

Number of Blocks and Finished Size
20 blocks   15½" x 15½"

Fabric Requirements
White   7¾ yards
Blue print   3 yards
Backing   7¾ yards*
Blue print for
    binding   ¾ yard
*Or 2¾ yards of 108"-wide backing fabric.

Other Materials
¼" cotton cording   8 yards

Pieces to Cut
White
    2 (11½" x 100") border
        strips
    2 (11½" x 84½") border
        strips
    20 (16") squares
Blue print**
    480 A
**From remaining fabric, make 2 (1" x 78"), 2 (1" x 63"), and 40 (1" x 15½") bias strips for appliqué.

Quilt Top Assembly
1. Fold 1 white square into quarters diagonally; finger-press. Unfold. Referring to *Appliqué Placement Diagram*, appliqué 24 As along pressed diagonal lines as shown.

To complete 1 block, fold under ¼" on each long edge of 2 bias strips. Press. Referring to *Appliqué Placement Diagram* and photograph, appliqué strips to block as shown, making sure

raw ends are turned under or hidden.

Repeat to make 20 blocks.

2. Join blocks in 5 rows of 4 blocks each. Join rows.

3. To make corded border, cut 2 (78"-long) and 2 (63"-long) pieces from cotton cording. Fold 1 (1" x 78") blue print strip in half; place 1 (78"-long) piece of cording inside fold. Using cording foot on sewing machine, baste strip over cording. Repeat for remaining pieces.

4. Place 1 (78"-long) cord on 1 side of quilt, aligning raw edges. Pin or baste in place. Place 1 (11½" x 100") white border on top of cord, aligning raw edges. Stitch through quilt top, border, and fabric edges of

cording. (Do not stitch through cord.)

Repeat for remaining side.

5. In same manner, join top and bottom borders with corded border, mitering corners.

Quilting
Quilt in-the-ditch around all appliquéd pieces. Quilt feathers in borders. Quilt *Feathered Wreath Quilting Pattern* between appliquéd pieces, and *Side Feather Quilting Pattern* inside corded border. Stipple-quilt background.

Finished Edges
Bind with straight-grain or bias binding made from blue print.

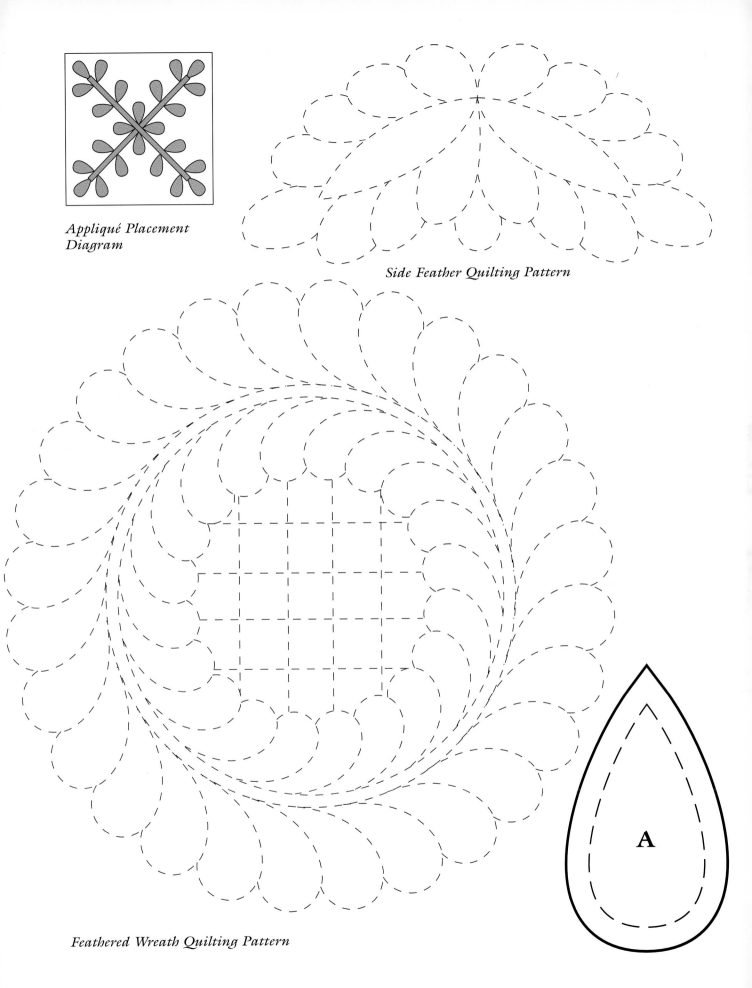

Appliqué Placement Diagram

Side Feather Quilting Pattern

Feathered Wreath Quilting Pattern

A

Starr Howell
Old Hickory, Tennessee

*S*tarr Howell loves everything about fabric. "It used to bother me when I would purchase a stack of different fabrics I liked but that didn't obviously go together," she says. "Someone would always ask me what I was going to do with all that. I like to wash it, fold it, cut it, and fondle it. I collect it. So I just tell them I'm a fabric collector!"

Starr usually has several quilts in progress at all times in order to enjoy the various stages of quiltmaking. "I start out making a block or two and let them talk to me for a couple of days. Some say nothing and go into the 'unfinished' basket, but most eventually go into a quilt." Some of her quilts may take years to complete, but Starr savors the whole process. "I'm not one to have to start and then finish a project right away," she says. "It doesn't bother me if it takes several years."

"Some people collect salt-and-pepper shakers, baseball cards, cars—I just collect fabric!"

In all, Starr considers herself a very fortunate person. "I am a wife, a mother of two daughters, grandmother of four granddaughters, and daughter and care-giver of my 91-year-old mother who lives with us and is a *quilter!*" she says. "Am I not blessed?"

Twirling Stars
1994

"I like stars of all kinds, and I like working with many fabrics," Starr says. "This quilt is the best of both."

Once she had completed the blocks, Starr arranged them on her wall until she found this pleasing setting.

Since she was going on vacation and planned to hand-piece the top, she labeled each block's position with an orange paper tag.

"As I put the top together, I left the tags in place," she says. "You guessed it! I spilled something on it and all the orange dye from the tags ran over the quilt top. I ended up replacing about 25 pieces. I still use tags on my blocks— but only *white* ones from now on!"

Twirling Stars

Finished Quilt Size
65" x 87"

Number of Blocks and Finished Size
43 blocks   7¾" x 7¾"

Fabric Requirements

Light blue	3½ yards
Dark blue	¾ yard
White	¾ yard
Light prints	43 scraps*
Medium prints	43 scraps*
Dark prints	43 scraps*
Backing	5½ yards
Blue for binding	¾ yard

*Scraps should measure at least 8" square. For most efficient piecing, a strip measuring 1" x 32" of each fabric is ideal.

Pieces to Cut

Light blue
    2 (4½" x 87½") border strips
    2 (4½" x 65½") border strips
    12 (3⅝" x 22") setting strips
    4 (3⅝" x 14½") setting strips
    2 (12⅞") squares**
    4 (12½") squares***
    68 B
    68 C

Dark blue
    16 (1¼" x 16") trim strips
    4 (1¼" x 17½") trim strips
    32 (1¼" x 9½") trim strips

White
    104 B
    104 C

**Cut each square in half diagonally for 4 corner triangles.

***Cut each square into quarters diagonally for 16 side triangles.

Quilt Top Assembly

1. To make 1 star block, select 1 light, 1 medium, and 1 dark print in coordinating shades. If possible, cut 1 (1" x 32") strip of each print. Otherwise, cut 8 (1" x 4") strips of each print. Join strips in order (light, medium, dark) along long edges. Press seams to 1 side. Place Template A over pieced strip, aligning dashed lines with seam lines. Cut 1 A along solid cutting line. Repeat to cut 8 As.

Referring to *Block Assembly Diagram,* join As, 4 light blue Bs, and 4 light blue Cs as shown to make 1 star block. Repeat to make 17 light blue star blocks.

2. Repeat Step 1, using white Bs and Cs, to make 1 white star block. Repeat to make 26 white star blocks.

3. Referring to *Quilt Top Assembly Diagram,* join blue star blocks as shown to make X-shaped center of quilt.

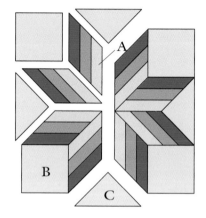

Block Assembly Diagram

4. Join light blue setting strips to edges of star blocks as shown in *Quilt Top Assembly Diagram,* mitering corners.

5. Join 1¼" x 16" dark blue trim strips to edges of setting strips, mitering corners.

6. Join white star blocks in 6 groups of 3 and 4 groups of 2 as shown in *Quilt Top Assembly Diagram.* Join groups to edges of quilt.

94

7. Join remaining dark blue trim strips to edges of white star blocks as shown, mitering corners.

8. Join side and corner triangles to edges of quilt.

9. Join 4½" x 87½" light blue border strips to sides of quilt. Join 4½" x 65½" light blue border strips to top and bottom of quilt, mitering corners.

Quilting

Quilt in-the-ditch around all As. Quilt vertical lines 1" apart across borders and backgrounds of star blocks. Quilt feathers in setting strips and triangles.

Finished Edges

Bind with straight-grain or bias binding made from light blue.

Quilt Top Assembly Diagram

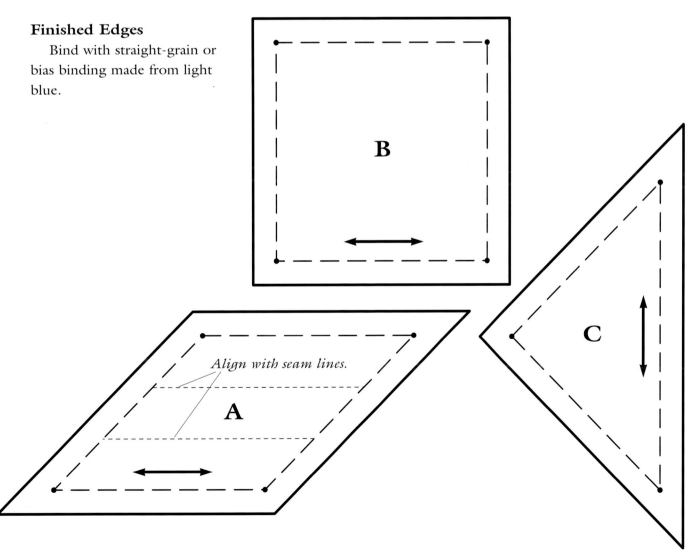

Bee Quilters

Minuet in Flowers

Carolina Vineyard

Door Country Christmas

Roses for Sunshine

San Fernando Valley Quilt Association
Granada Hills, California

Minuet in Flowers
1996

Based on an original design for counted cross-stitch by Renee Wamsat-Wells, *Minuet in Flowers* was made by members of Susie Schurman's mini-group as the 1996 opportunity quilt for the San Fernando Valley Quilt Association.

"Each year, the mini-groups submit designs for the fund-raising quilt to the guild, and the members vote for their favorite," Susie says. "The mini-group that presented the design coordinates the entire project, from purchasing the fabric to basting and quilting."

Renee, who is Susie's sister-in-law, is very pleased with the mini-group's interpretation of her design. "Susie translated my inked drawing into fabric," Renee says, "matching my marker colors exactly. She doggedly sought out the right fabrics and made sure that my vision of the quilt was accomplished as closely as possible!"

Susie's accomplishment, and those of the mini-group members, is even more impressive in light of other events going on at the same time. Many of the group members live in or near the area heavily damaged by the January 1994 Northridge earthquake; Susie's home was nearly destroyed. "Susie and her family lived in the master bedroom or camped in the backyard for almost two years, until repairs were completed," Renee says. "How she managed to survive—let alone oversee the work on the quilt—is amazing!"

Their efforts paid off handsomely for the Quilt Association; *Minuet in Flowers* was the largest money-maker ever for the guild. Now owned by Marilyn Haugen of Newbury Park, California, *Minuet in Flowers* continues to travel to quilt shows around the country, a testament to determination, skill, and inspired design.

Minuet in Flowers

Finished Quilt Size
106" x 106"

Number of Blocks and Finished Size

4 Block 1	15" x 15"
8 Block 2	12½" x 15"
9 Block 3	12½" x 12½"
4 Block 4	12½" x 12½"

Fabric Requirements

White	5½ yards
Yellow	¼ yard
Gold	¼ yard
Light blue print	¾ yard
Medium blue prints	1½ yards total
Dark blue prints	¼ yard
Darkest blue print	1¼ yards
Light pink print	¼ yard
Medium pink prints	¾ yard total
Dark pink print	2½ yards*
Red	¼ yard
Dark red	¼ yard
Light purple print	½ yard
Medium purple prints	¾ yard total
Dark purple print	¼ yard
Darkest purple	¼ yard
Green prints	1¼ yards total**
Check print	3¼ yards
Backing	9½ yards***
Gray for binding	¾ yard

*To cut borders in one lengthwise piece. To save fabric, buy ¾ yard and piece borders from crosswise strips.
**From 20" square of green print, make 280" of ¾"-wide bias. Press under ¼" on each long edge.
***Or 3¼ yards 108"-wide backing fabric.

The checked inner and outer borders in Minuet in Flowers *are actually composed of 4,132 white, pink, and gray squares—each measuring 0.8" square! To slightly simplify this very complex quilt, we've called for checked fabric for the borders. But if you wish to exactly reproduce the original, follow the photograph for color placement in making the borders.*

Note: Because of the complex cutting instructions for *Minuet in Flowers*, we are giving cutting and assembly instructions together for each block.

Block 1

1. To make 4 Block 1s, rotary-cut the following pieces from white: 4 (5") squares, 2 (11¼") squares, and 8 (5⅞") squares. Cut the 11¼" squares into quarters diagonally for 8 large triangles. Cut the 5⅞" squares in half diagonally for 16 small triangles.

From light blue, cut 4 (5⅞") squares. From medium blue, cut 6 (5⅞") squares. From dark blue, cut 4 (5⅞") squares. From darkest blue, cut 2 (5⅞") squares. Cut each square in half diagonally.

2. Referring to *Block 1 Assembly Diagram*, join 1 white square, 2 large white triangles, 4

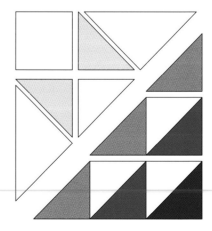

Block 1 Assembly Diagram

small white triangles, 2 light blue triangles, 3 medium blue triangles, 2 dark blue triangles, and 1 darkest blue triangle as shown to make 1 Block 1.

Repeat to make 4 Block 1s.

Block 2

1. To make 8 Block 2s, rotary-cut the following pieces from white and label with these letters: 8 (8" x 13") F, 16 (3¼" x 8") G, 8 (3" x 5½") H, 32 (1½" x 2½") I, 16 (1½" x 3½") J, and 112 (1½"-square) K.

From yellow, cut and label the following pieces: 48 (1½" x 3½") L and 8 (1½"-square) M.

From gold, cut and label the following pieces: 48 (1½" x 3½") N and 16 (1½" x 3½") O.

2. Referring to *Figure A*, join 2 Ks and 1 L as shown. Repeat to make 4.

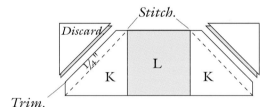

Figure A

Join 1 I and 2 Ns as shown in *Figure B* to make left side of bow. Repeat, reversing to make right side of bow.

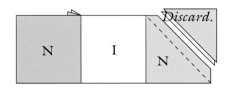

Figure B

Join 1 J and 1 N as shown in *Figure C* to make left side of ribbon. Repeat, reversing to make right side of ribbon.

Figure C

Join 1 L and 2 Ks as shown in *Figure D*. Repeat, reversing.

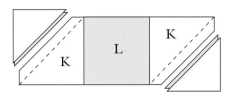

Figure D

Join 1 K and 1 O as shown in *Figure E* to make left side of streamer. Repeat, reversing to make right side of streamer.

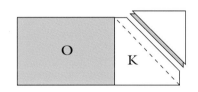

Figure E

3. Join pieced units with 1 F, 2 Gs, 1 H, 2 Is, and 1 M as

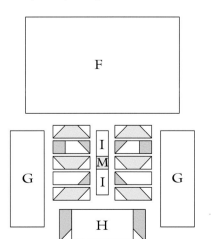

Block 2 Assembly Diagram

shown in *Block 2 Assembly Diagram*.

4. To make flowers, refer to photograph for color placement and cut the following pieces: 8 green print Cs, 8 green print C rev., 8 medium print Cs, 8 medium print C rev., and 8 dark print Ds.

Join 1 green print C, 1 green print C rev., 1 medium print C, 1 medium print C rev, and 1 dark print D as shown in *Flower Assembly Diagram*. Repeat to make 8 flowers.

Flower Assembly Diagram

5. Arrange flowers, 1 (20"-long) green print bias strip, and 3 (3"-long) green print bias strips on 1 F as shown in photograph. Appliqué flowers and bias strips to F to complete 1 Block 2.

6. Repeat Steps 2–5 to make 8 Block 2s.

Block 3

1. You will make 1 Block 3 from blue, 4 from pink, and 4 from purple. For all 9 Block 3s, rotary-cut the following pieces from white: 72 (3⅜") squares, cut in half diagonally for 144 half-square triangles, and 27 (3¾") squares, cut into quarters diagonally for 108 quarter-square triangles.

2. To make 1 blue Block 3, cut 2 (3¾") light blue squares and cut each into quarters diagonally for 8 quarter-square

101

triangles. From medium blue, cut 1 (3½") center square and 2 (3⅜") squares. Cut 3⅜" squares in half diagonally for 4 half-square triangles. From dark blue, cut 4 (3⅜") squares and cut each in half diagonally for 8 half-square triangles. From darkest blue, cut 2 (3⅜") squares and cut each in half diagonally for 4 half-square triangles. From medium pink, cut 4 (2½") corner squares.

3. To make 4 pink Block 3s, cut 8 (3¾") light purple squares and cut each into quarters diagonally for 32 quarter-square triangles. From medium pink, cut 1 (3½") center square and 8 (3⅜") squares. Cut 3⅜" squares in half diagonally for 16 half-square triangles. From red, cut 16 (3⅜") squares and cut each in half diagonally for 32 half-square triangles. From dark red, cut 8 (3⅜") squares and cut each in half diagonally for 16 half-square triangles. From medium purple, cut 16 (2½") corner squares.

4. To make 4 purple Block 3s, cut 8 (3¾") light purple squares and cut each into quarters-square triangles for 32 quarter-square triangles. From medium purple, cut 1 (3½") center square and 8 (3⅜") squares. Cut 3⅜" squares in half diagonally for 16 half-square triangles. From dark purple, cut 16 (3⅜") squares and cut each in half diagonally for 32 half-square triangles. From darkest purple, cut 8 (3⅜") squares and cut each in half diagonally for 16 half-square triangles. From

medium blue, cut 16 (2½") corner squares.

5. Referring to *Block 3 Assembly Diagram* and to photograph for color placement, join squares, half-square triangles, and quarter-square triangles as shown to make 1 blue Block 3, 4 pink Block 3s, and 4 purple Block 3s.

Block 3 Assembly Diagram

Block 4

1. To make 4 Block 4s, cut 4 (13") squares from white. Fold each square in half vertically and horizontally; finger-press to form appliqué placement guidelines. Unfold squares.

2. For flowers, refer to photograph for color placement and cut the following pieces: 4 yellow As, 16 gold Bs, 48 green print Cs, 48 green print C rev., 48 medium print Cs, 48 medium print C rev., and 48 dark print Ds.

3. Referring to *Center Flower Assembly Diagram*, join 1 A, 4 Bs, 4 green print Cs, 4 green print C rev., 4 medium print Cs, 4 medium print C rev., and 4 Ds as shown to make 1 center flower.

Center Flower Assembly Diagram

4. Referring to *Flower Assembly Diagram* on page 101, join 1 green print C, 1 green print C rev., 1 medium print C, 1 medium print C rev., and 1 D as shown to make 1 flower. Repeat to make 8 flowers.

5. Referring to *Block 4 Appliqué Placement Diagram*, appliqué center flower, 8 flowers, and 8 (2½"-long) green print bias strips to center of 1 white square as shown to complete 1 Block 4.

6. Repeat Steps 3–5 to make 4 Block 4s.

Block 4 Appliqué Placement Diagram

Sashing Strips

1. From white, cut 8 (3" x 15½") sashing strips and 24 (3"-square) sashing squares. Set aside.

2. For pieced sashing strips, cut 36 (3") squares and 72 (3⅜") squares from white. Cut 3⅜" squares in half diagonally for 144 half-square triangles.

3. You will make 4 blue pieced sashing strips, 16 pink, and 16 purple. From the following colors, cut the indicated number of 3⅜" squares: 4 light blue, 4 medium blue, 16 light pink, 16 medium pink, 16 light purple, and 16 medium purple. Cut each square in half diagonally.

4. Referring to photograph for color placement and to *Sashing Strip Assembly Diagram*, join 1 white square, 4 white half-square triangles, 2 light half-square triangles, and 2 medium half-square triangles as shown to make 1 sashing strip.

Sashing Strip Assembly Diagram

5. Repeat to make 4 blue, 16 pink, and 16 purple sashing strips.

Center Quilt Top Assembly

1. Referring to photograph for color placement and to *Quilt Top Assembly Diagram*, join blocks, sashing strips, and sashing squares in rows as shown. Join rows.

2. From check print, cut 2

Quilt Top Assembly Diagram

(3¾" x 78") border strips. Join to top and bottom edges of quilt. Cut 2 (3¾" x 84½") border strips. Join to sides of quilt, butting corners.

Pieced Border

1. From white, cut 68 (3⅜") squares and cut into quarters diagonally for 272 side triangles. From darkest blue, cut 2 (6¼") squares and cut each into quarters diagonally for 8 end triangles. From these colors, cut the following number of 2¼" squares: 64 light blue, 136 medium blue, and 192 darkest blue.

2. Referring to photograph for color placement and to *Pieced Border Assembly Diagram*, join 2 end triangles,

68 side triangles, 16 light blue squares, 34 medium blue squares, and 48 darkest blue squares as shown to make 1 pieced border. Repeat to make 4 borders.

Pieced Border Assembly Diagram

3. From dark pink, cut 8 (1½" x 84") border strips. Join 1 strip to each long edge of 1 pieced border. Repeat for remaining pieced borders.

Corner Blocks

1. To make 4 corner blocks, cut 12 E and 2 (6⅞") squares from white; cut each square in half diagonally for 4 large triangles. From dark pink, cut 8 (1½" x 7½") border strips. Cut 8 light purple Es, 12 medium purple Es, 8 dark purple Es, and 4 darkest purple Es.

2. Referring to photograph for color placement and to *Corner Block Assembly Diagram,* join 3 white Es, 3 medium purple Es, 2 dark purple Es, and 1 darkest purple E as shown. Join 1 dark pink strip to each short edge of 1 large white triangle, mitering corners. Join halves of

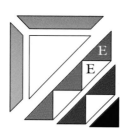

Corner Block Assembly Diagram

block. Appliqué 2 light purple Es to block as shown to complete 1 Corner Block.

Repeat to make 4 Corner Blocks.

Quilt Top Assembly

1. Join 2 pieced borders to top and bottom of quilt.

2. Join 1 Corner Block to each end of remaining pieced

borders. Join to sides of quilt, butting corners.

3. From check print, cut 2 (4½" x 98½") border strips. Join to top and bottom of quilt. Cut 2 (4½" x 106½") border strips. Join to sides of quilt, butting corners.

Quilting

Quilt around all pieced and appliquéd seam lines, or quilt as desired.

Finished Edges

Bind with straight-grain or bias binding made from gray.

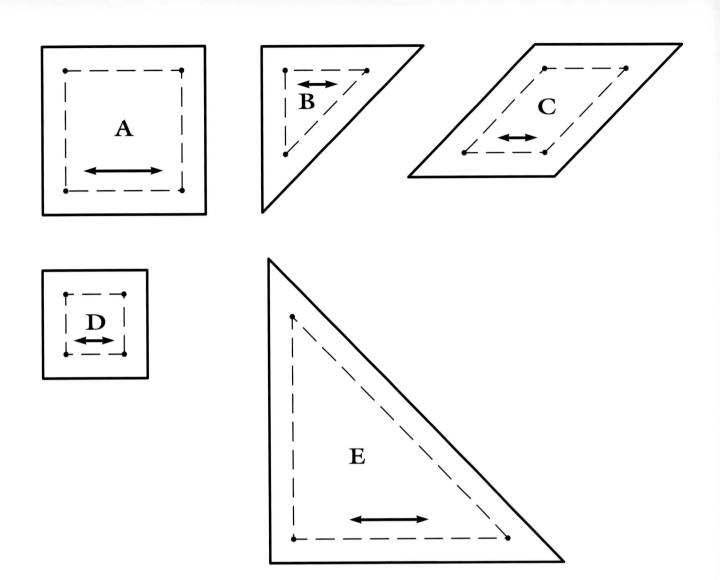

Members who worked on Carolina Vineyard: *Micki Batté, Nettie Blankenship, Jill Chirgotis, Rosemma Coppess, Carole Couse, Mary DeGroot, Judy Elliston, Jeanne Ferg, Mary Field, Patricia Gabriel, Shirley Henion, Sara Hill, Marge Hoppe, Cindy Lund, Janice Maddox, Susanne McCaskill, Bernice Mink, Sue Mueller, Marilyn Munson, Matey Rice, Barbara Swinea, Anne Vernon, Connie Williams.*

Asheville Quilt Guild
Asheville, North Carolina

The 200-member Asheville Quilt Guild emphasizes community service through its outreach and educational programs.

"We gave 26 quilts to the local hospice this year," says president Sara Hill. "We also sponsor Fiber Day at the Folk Arts Center, hold quilting classes in the local schools, and offer lectures on quilting to groups."

The guild also holds a quilt exhibit and competition each year, with cash prizes donated by Cranston Printworks, the maker of VIP fabrics.

Carolina Vineyard
1994

"Each year, one of the state quilt guilds sponsors the North Carolina Quilt Symposium and donates the fund-raising quilt," says Asheville Quilt Guild member Patricia Gabriel. "Early in 1993, my guild asked me to design the 1994 donation quilt. I constructed the top in October of 1993, and then 22 guild members hand-quilted for almost 200 hours to complete it!"

Trish wanted a scrap quilt, so she began by designing a background of blue squares with a large Carolina Lily block pieced in contrasting colors. "I added the smaller lilies for contrast in scale and translucence," she says. "As a secondary theme, I decided to celebrate the growth of the North Carolina wine industry by appliquéing grapes and vines over the top."

Carolina Vineyard

Finished Quilt Size
80" x 88"

Fabric Requirements

Blue prints	10½ yards total
Red prints*	½ yard total
Green prints	1½ yards total
Light prints	1 yard total
Backing	5 yards
Blue print for binding	¾ yard

*Includes red, pink, orange, gold, and purple prints in photograph.

Pieces to Cut

Blue prints
> 193 (4½") squares
> 17 (4⅞") squares**
> 18 B
> 10 C

Red prints***
> 1 (4½") square
> 19 (4⅞") squares**
> 37 B
> 18 C

Green prints
> 2 (4½") squares
> 5 (4⅞") squares**
> 9 A

Light prints
> 35 (4½") squares
> 17 (4⅞") squares**

**Cut each square in half diagonally to make 2 half-square triangles.
***Includes red, pink, orange, gold, and purple prints in photograph.

Quilt Top Assembly

1. From green print remaining after cutting squares, triangles, and As, make 200" of

Carolina Vineyard *is owned by Mrs. Paul Reeder of Oxford, North Carolina, and appears by her kind permission.*

¾"-wide bias. Fold under ¼" on each long edge; press. Set aside.

2. Referring to photograph and *Quilt Top Assembly Diagram* for color placement, join squares and half-square triangles as shown to make 18 rows. Join rows.

3. Referring to photograph for color arrangement, appliqué bias vines, leaves, and grapes to quilt top as shown.

4. To make border blocks, cut remaining blue prints into 1½"-wide strips. Join strips along long edges in groups of 13. From pieced strips, cut 19 (12½") squares. Cut each square into quarters diagonally as shown in *Border Block*

Cutting Diagram. Rotate 2 adjacent triangles and stitch together along long edges, as shown in *Border Block Assembly Diagram*, to make 1 border block. Repeat to make 38 border blocks.

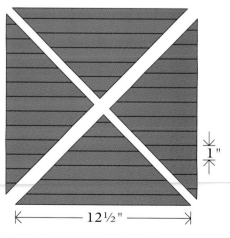

Border Block Cutting Diagram

Figure 1

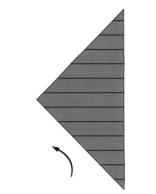

Figure 2

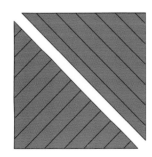

Figure 3

Figure 4
Border Block Assembly Diagram

5. To make top border, join 8 border blocks as shown in photograph. Join to top of quilt. Repeat to make and join bottom border.

6. In same manner, join 11 border blocks to make 1 side border. Repeat. Join to sides of quilt, butting corners.

Quilting

Quilt an overall fan pattern across entire quilt, or quilt as desired.

Finished Edges

Bind with straight-grain or bias binding made from remaining blue prints.

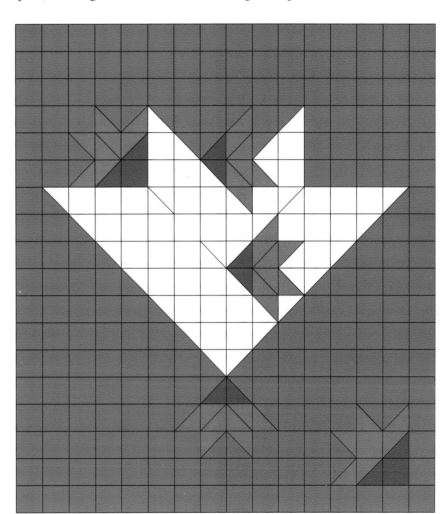

Quilt Top Assembly Diagram

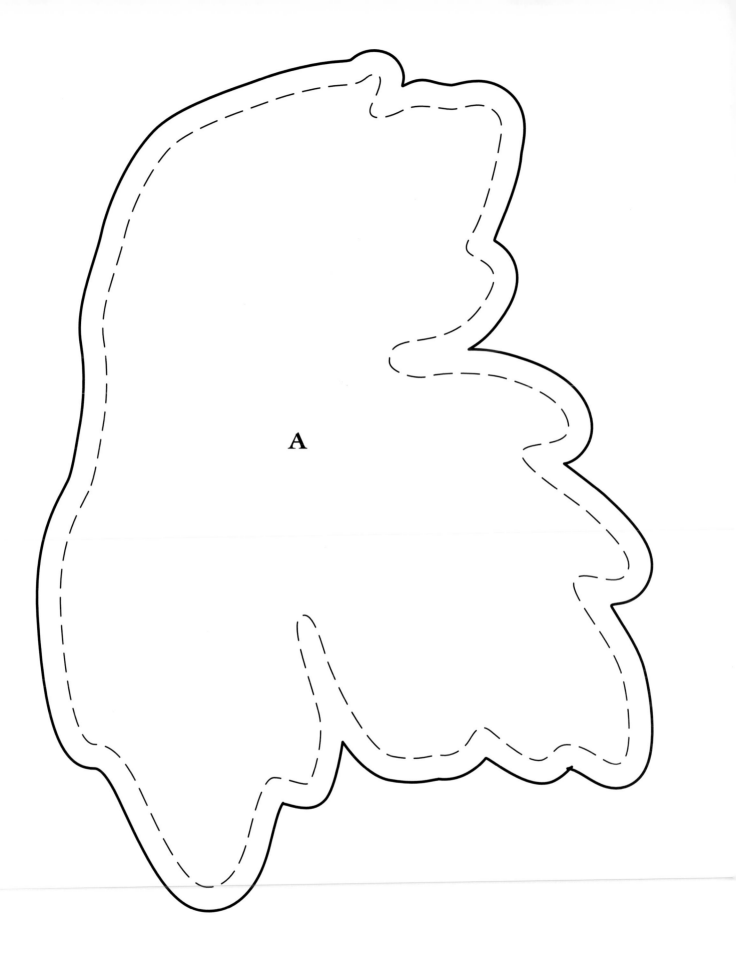

A

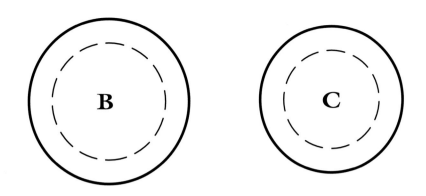

Darting Needles Quilt Guild
Neenah, Wisconsin

The Darting Needles, organized in 1982, now boasts almost 250 members. "Our skill levels range widely, and our members are interested in everything," says designer Linda Roy. "Show and Tell each month is incredible. It always takes up as much time as the guest speaker—sometimes more!"

Darting Needles members enjoy sharing their expertise with others, offering demonstrations to schools and other groups. They also donate quilts to local children's homes and organizations for families in need.

Door County Christmas
1995

"We hold a quilt show in every even year," says Linda. "In 1995, Janett McGinnis—one of the chairmen for the 1996 show—asked me to design an opportunity quilt that was a little special. Our goal was to make a quilt exceptional enough to be accepted into the juried American Quilters' Society show in Paducah."

Linda designed the quilt, chose the fabrics, and wrote appliqué instructions for the members. Dawn Schultz drew patterns, assembled kits for the center blocks, drafted and sewed the inner sashing strips, and marked the four outer borders. Linda assembled the completed blocks, added the outer borders, and quilted the entire piece in two and a half months.

"Working on a personal quilt of this nature brought our guild members closer together," Linda says.

Door County Christmas

Finished Quilt Size
75½" x 75½"

Number of Blocks and Finished Size
9 blocks   13½" x 13½"

Fabric Requirements

Light brown print	5½ yards
Dark brown print	4 yards
Dark green print	1¾ yards
Green print	1¼ yards
Christmas print	2¼ yards
Gold	¼ yard
Red prints	½ yard total
Backing	5 yards
Dark green print for binding	¾ yard

Other Materials
Embroidery floss or silk ribbon

Pieces to Cut

Light brown print
- 2 (28⅞") squares*
- 4 (14") squares
- 120 G
- 256 J
- 8 L
- 8 L rev.
- 56 N
- 16 O

Dark brown print
- 4 (2½" x 44") border strips
- 5 (14") squares
- 24 F
- 48 H
- 16 I
- 120 K
- 32 M
- 4 P

Dark green print
- 4 (1" x 44") border strips
- 52 A

Green print
- 156 E
- 52 (¾" x 7") bias strips**

Christmas print
- 4 (1½" x 76") border strips
- 13 B

Gold
- 13 C

Red prints
- 260 D

*Cut each in half diagonally for 4 corner triangles.
**Fold under ¼" on each long edge; press.

Door County Christmas *is owned by Raymond J. Pollen of Milwaukee, Wisconsin.*

Appliqué Placement Diagram

Quilt Top Assembly

1. Fold 1 light brown print square into quarters diagonally; finger-press. Unfold. Referring to *Appliqué Placement Diagram* and using creases as placement guidelines, appliqué 4 bias strips, 4 As, 1 B, 1 C, 8 Ds to form center flower, 12 Ds to form berries at end of bias strips, and 12 Es to block as shown. To complete block, embroider French knots in center of flower, covering raw edges of Ds.

Repeat to make 4 light brown and 5 dark brown print blocks.

114

2. To make 1 sashing strip, join 2 Fs, 10 Gs, and 4 Hs as shown in *Sashing Assembly Diagram*. Repeat to make 12 sashing strips.

F G H

Sashing Assembly Diagram

3. Referring to photograph for color placement, join blocks with sashing strips in 3 rows of 3 blocks. Join rows.

4. Join dark green border strips to edges of quilt, mitering corners. Join dark brown print border strips to edges of quilt, trimming corners as shown in *Quilt Top Assembly Diagram*. Join 1 corner triangle to each corner of quilt.

5. Referring to Step 1, appliqué 1 flower in each corner triangle.

6. To make 1 narrow pieced border, join 2 Is, 32 Js, and 15 Ks as shown in *Narrow Border Assembly Diagram*. Repeat to make 8 narrow borders.

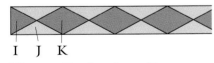

I J K

Narrow Border Assembly Diagram

7. To make 1 wide pieced border, join 2 Ls, 2 Ls rev., 8 Ms, and 14 Ns as shown in *Wide Border Assembly Diagram*. Repeat to make 4 wide borders.

L rev.

M

L N

Wide Border Assembly Diagram

8. Join 1 narrow border to each edge of 1 wide border. Repeat to make 4 borders.

9. Join 1 border to top and bottom of quilt.

10. To make 1 side border, join 4 Os and 1 P as shown in *Quilt Top Assembly Diagram* to make 1 corner square. Repeat to make 2. Join 1 square to each end of 1 border. Join to 1 side of quilt, butting corners.

Repeat for second side border.

11. Join Christmas print border strips to edges of quilt, mitering corners.

Quilting

Quilt in-the-ditch around all appliquéd pieces and pieces in sashing and borders. Quilt background with 1" crosshatch pattern.

Finished Edges

Bind with straight-grain or bias binding made from dark green print.

O

P

Quilt Top Assembly Diagram

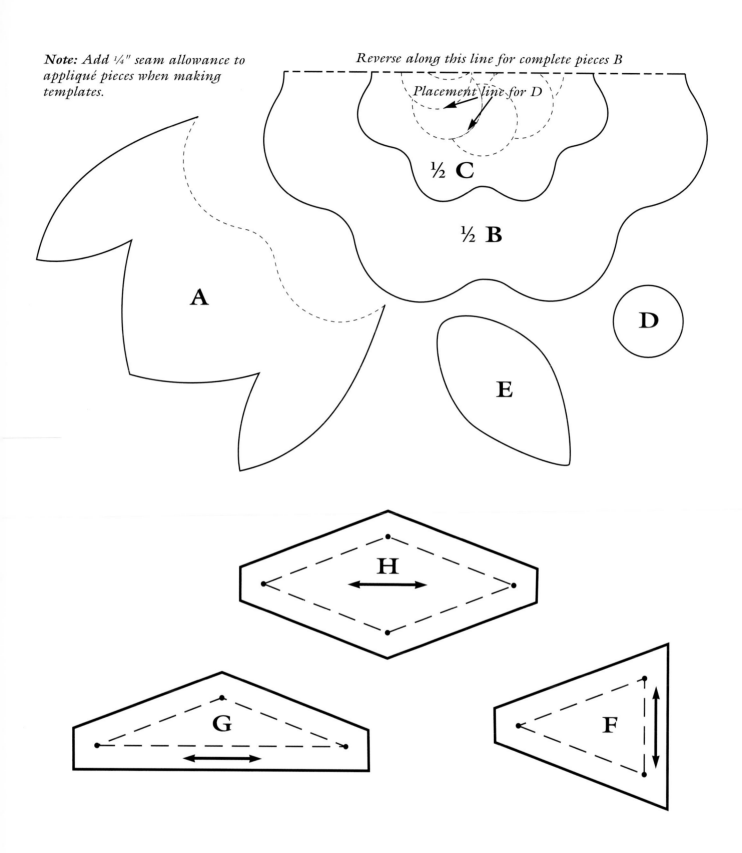

Note: Add ¼" seam allowance to appliqué pieces when making templates.

Reverse along this line for complete pieces B

Placement line for D

½ C

½ B

A

D

E

H

G

F

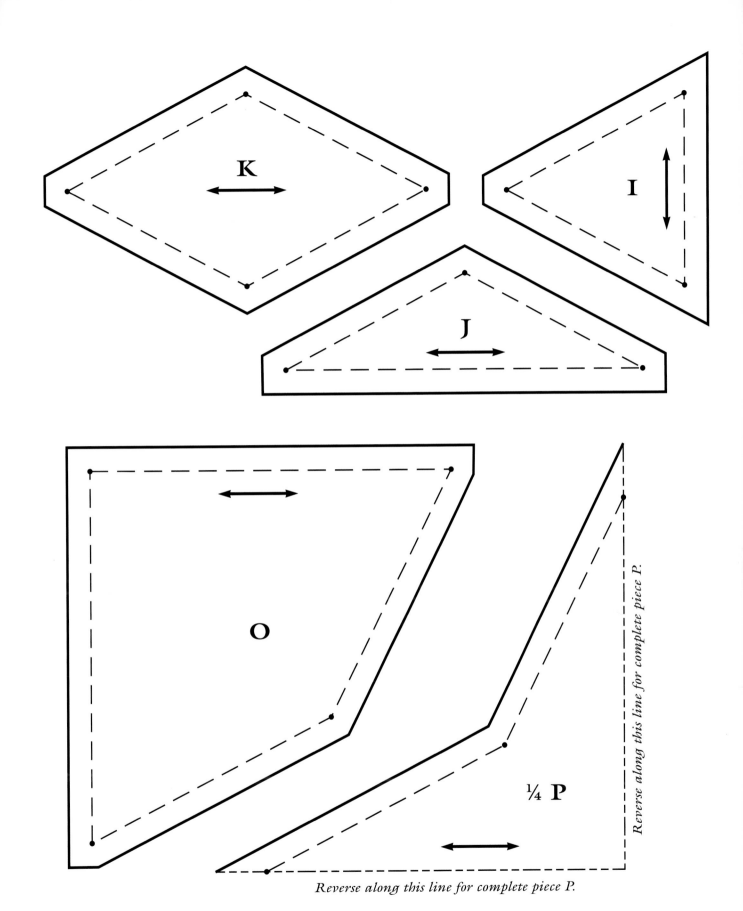

K

I

J

O

¼ P

Reverse along this line for complete piece P.

Reverse along this line for complete piece P.

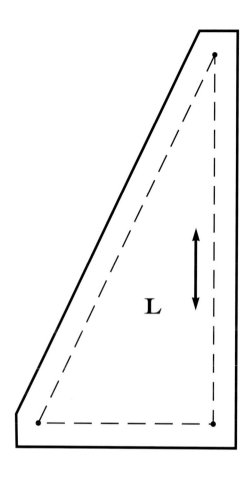

L

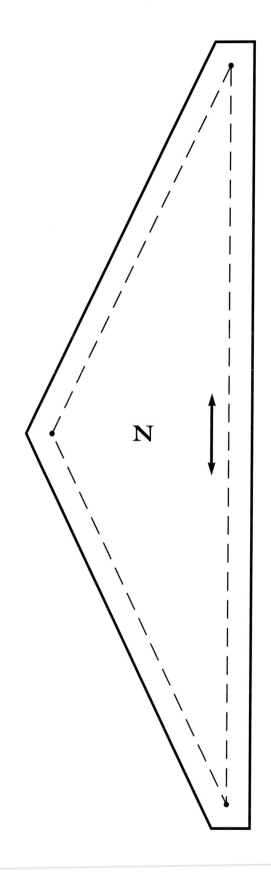

N

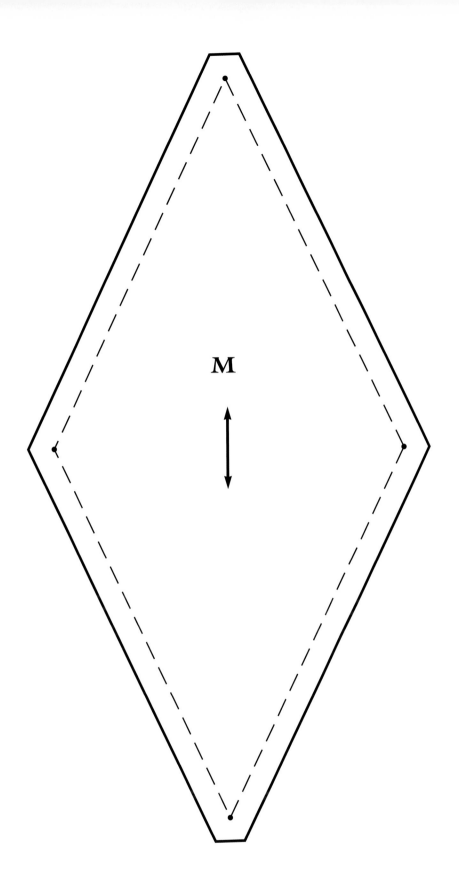

M

Quilt 'n' Patch Quilters
Toledo, Ohio

Back row, left to right: Kay Langsdorf, Georgia Huebner, Diane Walls, Jane Gruber.
Middle row, left to right: Bernadine Valasek, Kay Wilcox, Mary Gallaway, Mary Clark.
Front row, left to right: Mary Lou Forsee, Marcia Arnett.

Toledo, Ohio, is the home of a very special place—the Sunshine Children's Home, for children with severe medical infirmities—and a very special group of ladies—the Quilt 'n' Patch Quilters.

"We formed the group from students of a class at the Quilt 'n' Patch Quilt Shop," says founding member Mary Gallaway. "I had volunteered at the Sunshine Home, so it seemed natural for us to donate a small quilt to their first annual auction in 1976. Almost every year since then, we've contributed a quilt to their fund-raiser. We're always delighted when the generosity of a purchaser helps to fund the challenging work of the Sunshine Home."

Roses for Sunshine
1996

An adaptation of an antique Rose of Sharon quilt, *Roses for Sunshine* took the Quilt 'n' Patch Quilters almost two years to complete. "We meet as the need arises," Mary says, "not on a regular basis, until the quilt is in the frame and the deadline is approaching. We do work better under pressure!"

The quilt won First Prize for Group Quilts at the 1996 show held by the RSVP Quilters of Monroe County, and an Honorable Mention in Group Quilts at the 1996 American Quilters' Society show in Paducah.

Roses for Sunshine

Finished Quilt Size
90" x 108"

Number of Blocks and Finished Size

12 blocks   20" x 20"

Fabric Requirements

White	6½ yards
Green	4¼ yards
Dark red	3 yards
Medium red prints	1¼ yards total
Backing	8¼ yards*
Green for binding	1 yard

*Or 2¾ yards 108"-wide fabric.

Pieces to Cut

White
- 12 (20½") squares
- 2 (8½" x 94½") border strips
- 2 (8½" x 76½") border strips

Green
- 2 (6½" x 108½") border strips
- 2 (6½" x 90½") border strips
- 2 (1" x 95½") border strips
- 2 (1" x 77½") border strips
- 1 (30") square for bias
- 48 A
- 240 D

Dark red
- 2 (1" x 96½") border strips
- 2 (1" x 78½") border strips
- 12 B
- 64 E

Medium red prints
- 12 C
- 136 E

Quilt Top Assembly

1. From 30" square of green, make 60 (¾" x 8") and 60 (¾" x 7") bias strips. Fold under ¼"

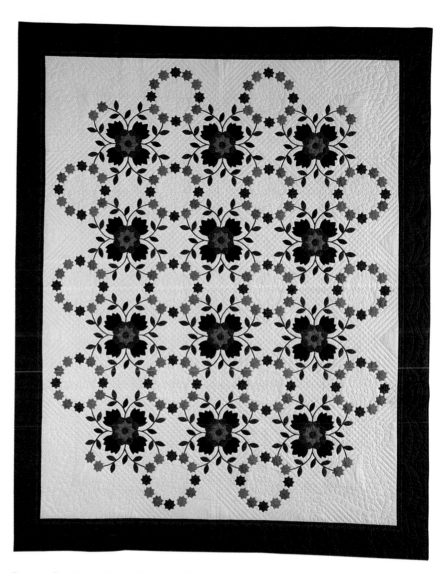

Roses for Sunshine *is owned by Katherine Frey of Archbold, Ohio.*

on each long edge; press. Set aside.

2. To make 1 block, fold 1 white square into quarters diagonally; finger-press. Unfold. Referring to *Appliqué Placement Diagram*, appliqué 4 (7"-long) bias strips, 4 (8"-long) bias strips, 4 As, 1 B, 1 C, 20 Ds, and 8 medium red print Es to square, in that order.

Repeat to make 12 blocks.

3. Join blocks in 4 rows of 3 blocks each, as shown in *Quilt Top Assembly Diagram*. Join rows.

Appliqué Placement Diagram

4. Join 6½" x 76½" white border strips to top and bottom of quilt. Join remaining border strips to sides of quilt, mitering corners.

5. Referring to photograph for placement, appliqué remaining Es to borders of quilt and across block seams as shown.

6. Join 1"-wide green borders to edges of quilt, mitering corners.

7. Join 1"-wide red borders to edges of quilt, mitering corners.

8. Join 6"-wide green borders to edges of quilt, mitering corners.

Quilting

Quilt in-the-ditch around all appliquéd pieces and borders. Quilt *Wreath Quilting Pattern* in centers of star circles. Quilt background with 1" crosshatch pattern as shown in photograph, or quilt as desired.

Finished Edges

Bind with straight-grain or bias binding made from green.

Quilt Top Assembly Diagram

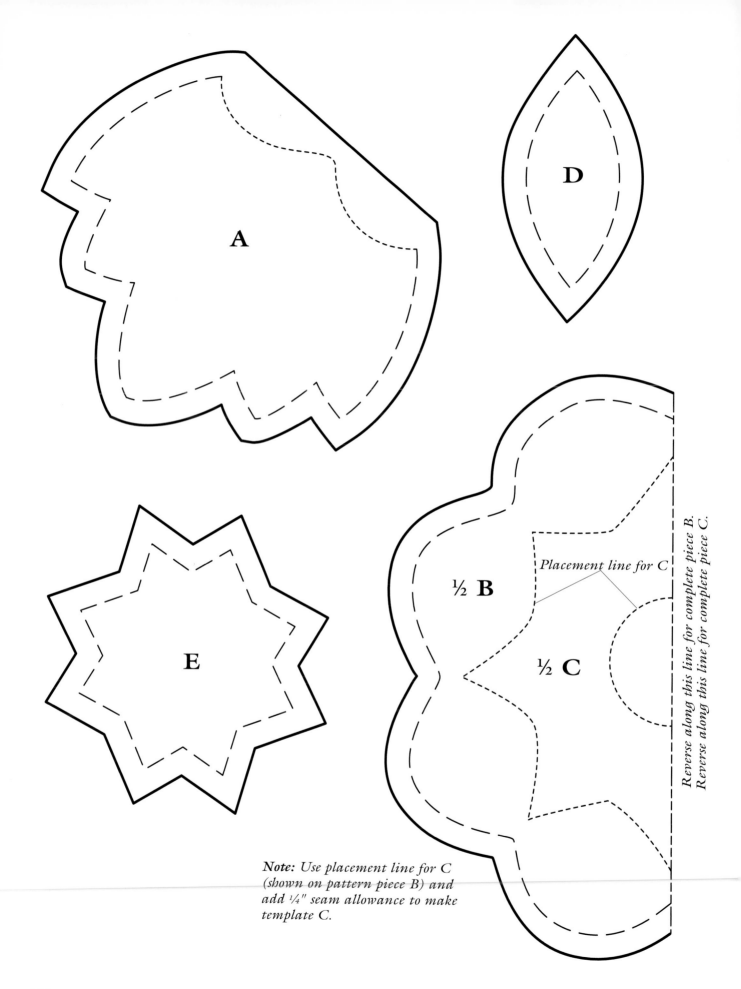

A

D

½ B

½ C

Placement line for C

E

Reverse along this line for complete piece B.
Reverse along this line for complete piece C.

Note: *Use placement line for C (shown on pattern piece B) and add ¼" seam allowance to make template C.*

Wreath Quilting Pattern

Designer Gallery

Chickens Who Run
with the Wolves

An Introduction to
Linear Algebra

Simple Gifts

Jacobeana

Cosmic Escher

Maui Boy

Tadaima

128

Betsy Cannon
Aurora, Colorado

*B*etsy Cannon never really began quilting; she just ended up there after years of experimenting with embroidery. "My stitches just got more regular," she says, "and I started to put batting between the layers. Next thing I knew, I was quilting."

"I try to be open to the whimsical in life and interpret that in my quilts."

Her quilt style is as spontaneous and candid as Betsy herself. "I'm not a precise person," she says. "I'm not temperamentally suited to make a pieced quilt." She loves textured appliqué, with lots of loose threads, buttons, sequins, paint, and beads on her quilts. "I'm inspired by all sorts of things," she says. "Silly songs, children's stories, cartoons. I try to be open to the humorous and whimsical things in life and interpret that in my quilts."

Chickens Who Run with the Wolves
1994

"I've always liked chickens," says Betsy Cannon. "They are a funny shape, they make cute little sounds, and best of all, they have such wonderful *legs!*"

At the time Betsy began this quilt, a book called *Women Who Run with the Wolves* was on the best-seller list. "I'd been thinking about the quilt and had already determined that it would have very flamboyant chickens," Betsy says. "It occurred to me that my chickens, with their sequins and fluffy feathers, would be chickens who would run with wolves!"

This quilt is the only one ever received at Oxmoor House along with a note from its inhabitants. The "letter from the chickens," complete with stamped chicken-foot signatures, requested that we fluff up their nests before we took their picture so that they'd look their best in photography!

"Chicken houses usually have flies, right?" Betsy asks. So she added several beaded flies to the chicken-wire quilted background. "I liked the idea of having three-dimensional elements in the quilt."

Christine Curtis
Seattle, Washington

*A*bout seven years ago, one of Christine Curtis's hobbies led directly to another.

"Sometimes I go for weeks at a time without quilting. But once I start a quilt, I want to spend every waking moment on it."

"I wanted to turn my running T-shirts into a quilt," she says. "I took a beginning quilting class as a local shop, and it was a revelation. I've been making clothes since I was 8, but suddenly I could choose colors, style, size; a quilt doesn't have to fit or look good on me!"

An Introduction to Linear Algebra marks a departure in quilt style for Christine. "I like to make old-fashioned geometric quilts in unusual colors," she says. "Most of my quilts are bed covers. The combination of beauty and practicality is very appealing to me."

But she had so much fun designing and making her last two original wall hangings that she just might keep on in this direction. "I quilt for myself," she says firmly, "for the satisfaction I derive from it. Quilting has definitely enriched my life."

An Introduction to Linear Algebra
1996

Christine made *An Introduction to Linear Algebra* for her husband, a professor of mathematics, to hang in his office. "This design was on the cover of one of his textbooks a couple of years ago," she says. "He kept leaving it all over the house, and I must have picked it up again and again for weeks before I really looked at the book and realized: Those are houses. I could make a quilt." And so she did, foundation-piecing the houses and the letters from bright, happy fabrics.

The houses, Professor Curtis tells us, are a visual representation of what happens when points and lines are transformed by matrix algebra. The original design graced the cover of *An Introduction to Linear Algebra,* by Professor Gilbert Strang.

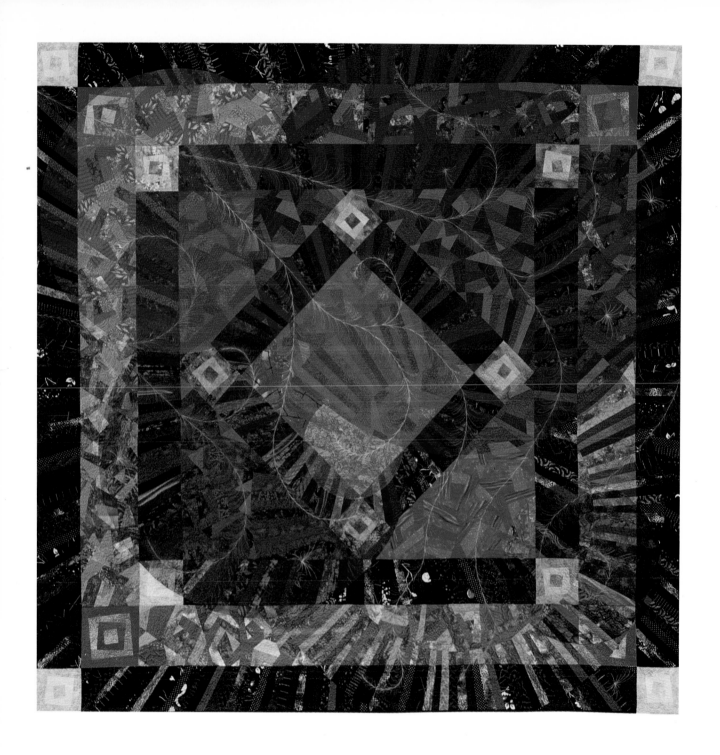

Ricky Tims
St. Louis, Missouri

Professional musician Ricky Tims came to quilting in an unusual way.

"In the summer of 1991, my 83-year-old widowed grandmother married her 87-year-old heartthrob," he says. "Her new home already had a sewing machine, so she gave her 1956 Kenmore to me."

"Quilts endure as reminders of quilters' lives, hopes, and dreams."

Not knowing any-thing about sewing, Ricky considered how best to use her gift. "I thought about making a shirt," he says, "but I thought it would be too difficult. So I decided to make something easier—a quilt!"

That first sampler quilt, made from traditional patterns he found in a book, was only the beginning. He almost immediately began designing original patterns and working out techniques to realize those designs. "I draw up a design using that particular method, and crank out a small quilt as quickly as possible," he says. "When people ask how I can be so productive, I don't know what to say. The determination and drive are present in all of us."

Simple Gifts
1996

When Ricky adapts a technique for one of his quilts, he adapts it in a *big* way!

For the 90" x 90" *Simple Gifts,* Ricky drew the entire design onto paper, full-size, and then pieced directly onto the paper. "Transparent color circles overlay a traditional Amish Diamond in a Square," Ricky says. "It is machine-quilted with 18 different colors of thread in free-form feather plumes." And not content with that, Ricky pieced another full-size Diamond in a Square on the back. (The back is shown on pages 126 and 127.)

The title reflects Ricky's other passion, music. *Simple Gifts* is the title of a well-known Shaker liturgical song, popularized by its use in Aaron Copland's ballet *Appalachian Spring.*

Sandra Ann Dockstader
Northfield, Minnesota

*S*andra Dockstader fell in love with quilting during the Bicentennial quilt revival. "I found a few quilt pictures in books," she says, "and I started teaching myself through trial and error."

Throughout her teenage years, she made quilts. But it wasn't until she married and moved to Minnesota that she really became serious about it. "After we moved in and got settled, I met others who liked to quilt, and I was hooked," she says. "I started working on several quilts at a time. I fell in love with appliqué and began working on Baltimore Album style quilts."

In the past few years, Sandra has moved toward original appliqué designs in both floral patterns and stained-glass designs based on the works of Louis Comfort Tiffany. Although she has developed a series of classes based on her own timesaving methods of machine appliqué, Sandra says that traditional hand appliqué is still her first love. "Flowers and nature are the basis for many of my designs," she says. "The possibilities are unlimited!"

Jacobeana
1995

"I love calla lilies," Sandra says. "I grew some to use at my wedding, and I still plant some of those same bulbs each spring."

Sandra looked for a pleasing calla lily quilt pattern for a number of years, but all that she found seemed stiff, too simplified, or had other flowers in the design. "I finally drew my own," she says. "I stayed with simple colors, so I could make the flowers more elaborate and add curves and graceful leaves."

She also designed the background quilting pattern, basing it on a combination of a traditional feather plume and a leaf shape from Jacobean appliqué.

"My grandmother's name was Jacobeana," Sandra says, "so the Jacobean theme seemed to fit. I named the quilt after her."

Sandra used fine-point fabric markers to add definition to the throats of the flower trumpets.

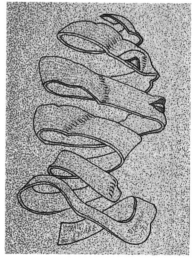

Deborah adapted a well-known Escher drawing to create the signature block on the quilt's back.

Deborah C. Little
Alva, Florida

Deborah Little learned to sew at the age of 10, and made countless doll clothes and clothes for herself and her family before beginning to quilt about 10 years ago. "From a report on my family history, I learned several years ago that my great-great-grandfather, an immigrant from Russia,

"I wonder if it's possible to hand down a love of sewing in the genes?"

had made his living as tailor to the governor of Illinois," Deborah says. "At the time, I was also employed as a tailor at a fashionable department store!"

Deborah sees quilting as a natural progression for people who love to sew. "It's a move from the making of functional items to the growth of pure creativity and expression," she says. "Quilting is the part of me that is the true me."

Cosmic Escher
1996

In the summer of 1995, Deborah read about a contest called "Quilts: Artistic Inspirations," which asked for original quilts based upon the color palette of a decorative artist or painter. "I was at a point in my quilting life that I wanted a challenge," she says. "I knew immediately that I would choose graphic artist M.C. Escher and that I would use the Kaufman Pointillist Palette fabrics."

Deborah worked out the complex swirling earth pattern on computer and carefully incorporated the shadings of her chosen fabric into the design. "The piece did indeed turn out to be a challenge," she says, "but I was pleased with the end product."

Although *Cosmic Escher* did not place in the original contest, it has won several awards since then, including First Place and Best of Show at the 1996 show in Naples, Florida.

Charlene Hughes
Pukalani, Maui, Hawaii

Charlene Hughes is one of the sunniest people you could ever meet—one of those rare souls who doesn't let obstacles bother her.

"We live in Paradise, but Paradise has very few quilt shops!" she says. "I recently used some fabric that I batiked 20 years ago. If I can't find what I want, I'll dye it myself or trade for it—anything except my cats or my husband (and the husband is negotiable!)"

When she decided to join a quilt guild and found that there was no group on Maui, she joined the Hawaii Quilt Guild in Honolulu. "Flying inter-island is expensive," she says. "I told my husband maybe I should just move there. I'd write faithfully, and he could send money!" Since Bruce didn't agree, Charlene decided to start her own guild on Maui.

"I was determined that this would work, even if only two or three other quilters were interested," she says. "Instead, 40 excited people showed up at the organizational meeting, and we now have almost a hundred members!"

Maui Boy
1996

Charlene made this little treasure as a sample for a class she teaches on mola quilting, a reverse-appliqué technique based on the work of the Cuna Indian women of the San Blas Islands off the coast of Panama. "I adore the folk-art look," she says. "This design is based on one of my cats, Attila. He and Genghis are very creative, and they enjoy helping me quilt. 'What, are we starting a new quilt?' they ask, curling up for a nap."

"Attila doesn't like Maui Boy," *Charlene says. "Apparently, he doesn't think it accurately reflects how handsome he really is!"*

Tadaima *is owned by Dr. and Mrs. J. Mark Scearce, and appears by their kind permission.*

Tadaima
1995

What do music and quilting have in common? In Hawaii, a piece called *Tadaima.*

Charlene designed and made the quilt *Tadaima* (Japanese for "I'm home") for the Hawaii Quilt Guild's annual quilt show in May of 1996. "At the show, a young man told me he loved my quilt and wanted to buy it," Charlene says. "Of course, I didn't believe him!"

The young man was Dr. Mark Scearce, a professor of music at the University of Hawaii and director of Chamber Music Hawaii's Festival of Contemporary Music. He loved the quilt so much that his wife tracked Charlene down after the show and bought *Tadaima* as a gift for Mark's birthday.

In response to the quilt's beauty, Dr. Scearce wrote a musical work for flute, viola,

and harp, also called *Tadaima,* which premiered at the Festival of Contemporary Music in February of 1997. "I hope that the musical work also communicates some of the same peace and tranquility," he says.

QUILT SMART WORKSHOP
A Guide to Quiltmaking

Preparing Fabric

Before cutting out any pieces, be sure to wash and dry your fabric to preshrink it. All-cotton fabrics may need to be pressed before cutting. Trim selvages from the fabric before you cut your pieces.

Making Templates

Before you can make one of the quilts in this book, you must make templates from the printed pattern pieces given. Quilters have used many materials to make templates, including cardboard and sandpaper. Transparent template plastic, available at craft supply and quilt shops, is durable, see-through, and easy to use.

To make templates using plastic, place the plastic sheet on the printed page and trace the pattern piece, using a laundry marker or permanent fine-tip marking pen. For machine piecing, trace along the outside solid (cutting) line. For hand piecing, trace along the inside broken (stitching) line. Cut out the template along the traced line. Label each template with the pattern name, letter, grain line arrow, and match points (corner dots).

Marking and Cutting Fabric

Place the template facedown on the wrong side of the fabric and mark around the template with a sharp pencil. Move the template (see next two paragraphs) and continue marking pieces; mark several before you stop to cut.

If you will be piecing your quilt by machine, the pencil lines represent the cutting lines. Leave about ¼" between pieces as you mark. Cut along the marked lines.

For hand piecing, the pencil lines are the seam lines. Leave at least ¾" between marked lines for seam allowances. Add ¼" seam allowance around each piece as you cut. Mark match points (corner dots) on each piece.

Hand Piecing

To hand piece, place two fabric pieces together with right sides facing. Insert a pin in each match point of the top piece. Stick the pin through both pieces and check to be sure that it pierces the match point on the bottom piece (*Figure 1*). Adjust the pieces if necessary to align the match points. (The raw edges of the two pieces may not be exactly aligned.) Pin the pieces securely together.

Sew with a running stitch of 8 to 10 stitches per inch. Checking your stitching as you go to be sure that you are stitching in the seam line of both pieces, sew from match point to match point. To make sharp corners, begin and end the stitching exactly at the match point; do not stitch into the seam allowances. When joining units where several seams come together, do not sew over seam allowances; sew through them at the point where all seam lines meet (*Figure 2*).

Always press both seam allowances to one side. Pressing the seam open, as in dressmaking, may leave gaps between the stitches through which quilt batting may beard. Press seam allowances toward the darker fabric whenever you can. When four or more seams meet at one point, such as at the corner of a block, press all the seams in a "swirl" in the same direction to reduce bulk (*Figure 3*).

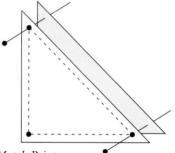

1—*Aligning Match Points*

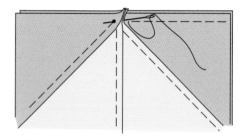

2—*Joining Units*

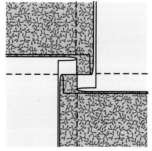

3—*Pressing Intersecting Seams*

Machine Piecing

To machine piece, place two fabric pieces together with right sides facing. Align match points as described under "Hand Piecing" and pin the pieces together securely.

Set your stitch length at 12 to 15 stitches per inch. At this setting, you will not need to backstitch to lock seam beginnings and ends. Use a presser foot that gives a perfect

¼" seam allowance, or measure ¼" from the sewing machine needle and mark that point on the presser foot with nail polish or masking tape.

Chain-piece sections, stitching edge to edge, to save time when sewing similar sets of pieces *(Figure 4)*. Join the first two pieces as usual. At the end of the seam, do not backstitch, cut the thread, or lift the presser foot. Instead, sew a few stitches off the fabric. Place the next two pieces and continue stitching. Keep sewing until all the sets are joined. Then cut the sets apart.

Press seam allowances toward the darker fabric. When you join blocks or rows, press the seam allowances of the top piece in one direction and the seam allowances of the bottom piece in the opposite direction to help ensure that the seams will lie flat *(Figure 5)*.

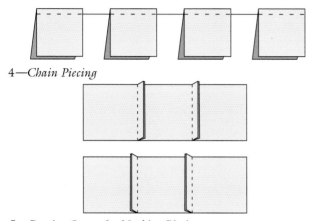

4—*Chain Piecing*

5—*Pressing Seams for Machine Piecing*

Hand Appliqué

Hand appliqué is the best way to achieve the look of traditional appliqué. However, using freezer paper, which is sold in grocery stores, can save a lot of time because it eliminates the need for hand basting the seam allowances.

Make templates without seam allowances. Trace the template onto the *dull* side of the freezer paper and cut the paper on the marked line. Make a freezer-paper shape for each piece to be appliquéd. Pin the freezer-paper shape, with its *shiny side up,* to the *wrong side* of your fabric. Following the paper shape and adding a scant ¼" seam allowance, cut out the fabric piece. Do not remove the pins. Using the tip of a hot, dry iron, press the seam allowance to the shiny side of the freezer paper. Be careful not to touch the shiny side of the freezer paper with the iron. Remove the pins.

Pin the appliqué shape in place on the background fabric. Use one strand of sewing thread in a color to match the appliqué shape. Using a very small slipstitch *(Figure 6)* or blindstitch *(Figure 7)*, appliqué the shape to the background fabric.

After your stitching is complete, cut away the background fabric behind the appliqué shape, leaving ¼" seam allowance. Separate the freezer paper from the fabric with your fingernail and pull gently to remove it.

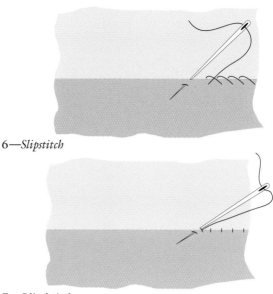

6—*Slipstitch*

7—*Blindstitch*

Mitering Borders

Mitered borders take a little extra care to construct. First, measure your quilt. Cut two border strips to fit the shorter of two opposite sides, plus the width of the border plus 2". Now center the measurement for the shorter side on one border strip and place a pin at each end of the measurement. Match the pins on the border strip to the corners of the longer side of the quilt. Join the border strip to the quilt, easing the quilt to fit between the pins and stopping ¼" from each corner of the quilt *(Figure 8)*. Join the remaining cut strip to the opposite end of the quilt. Cut and join the remaining borders in the same manner. Press seams to one side. Follow *Figures 9 and 10* to miter corners.

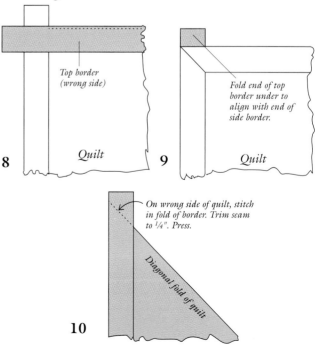

8 *Top border (wrong side)* *Quilt*

9 *Fold end of top border under to align with end of side border.* *Quilt*

10 *On wrong side of quilt, stitch in fold of border. Trim seam to ¼". Press.* *Diagonal fold of quilt*

Mitering Borders

Marking Your Quilt Top

After the quilt top is completed, it should be thoroughly pressed and then marked with quilting designs. The most popular methods for marking use stencils or templates. Both can be purchased, or you can make your own. Use a silver quilter's pencil for marking light to medium fabrics and a white artist's pencil on dark fabrics. Lightly mark the quilt top with your chosen quilting designs.

Making a Backing

While some fabric and quilt shops sell 90" and 108" widths of backing fabric, the instructions in *Great American Quilts* give backing yardage based on 45"-wide fabric. When using 45"-wide fabric, all quilts wider than 42" will require a pieced backing. For quilts whose width measures between 42" and 80", purchase an amount of fabric equal to two times the desired length of the unfinished quilt backing. (The unfinished quilt backing should be at least 3" larger on all sides than the quilt top.)

The backing fabric should be of a type and color that is compatible with the quilt top. Percale sheets are not recommended because they are tightly woven and difficult to hand-quilt through.

A pieced backing for a bed quilt should have three panels. The three-panel backing is recommended because it tends to wear better and lie flatter than the two-panel type, the center seam of which often makes a ridge down the center of the quilt. Begin by cutting the fabric in half widthwise *(Figure 11)*. Open the two lengths and stack them, with right sides facing and selvages aligned. Stitch along both selvage edges to create a tube of fabric *(Figure 12)*. Cut down the center of the top layer of fabric *only* and open the fabric flat *(Figure 13)*.

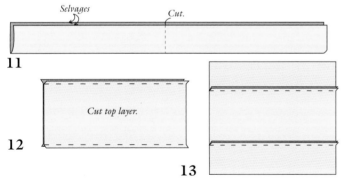

Making a Three-Panel Backing

Layering and Basting

Prepare a working surface to spread out the quilt. Place the backing on the working surface right side down. Unfold the batting and place it on top of the backing. Smooth any wrinkles or lumps in the batting.

Lay the quilt top right side up on top of the batting and backing. Make sure the backing and quilt top are aligned. Knot a long strand of sewing thread and use a darning needle for basting. Begin basting in the center of your quilt and baste out toward the edges. The stitches should cover an ample amount of the quilt so that the quilt layers do not shift during quilting. Inadequate basting can result in puckers and folds on the back and front of the quilt.

Hand Quilting

Hand quilting can be done with the quilt in a hoop or in a floor frame. It is best to start quilting in the middle of your quilt and work out toward the edges.

Most quilters use a very thin, short needle called a "between." Betweens are available in sizes 7 to 12, with 7 being the longest and 12 the shortest. If you are a beginning quilter, try a size 7 or 8. Because betweens are so much shorter than other hand-sewing needles, they may feel awkward at first. As your skill increases, try switching to a smaller needle to help you make smaller stitches.

Quilting thread, heavier and stronger than ordinary sewing thread, is available in a wide variety of colors. But if color matching is critical and you can't find the color you need, you may substitute cotton sewing thread. We suggest you coat it with beeswax before quilting to prevent it from tangling and knotting.

To begin, thread your needle with an 18" to 24" length and make a small knot at one end. Insert the needle into the top of the quilt approximately ½" from the point you want to begin quilting. Do not take the needle through all three layers, but stop it in the batting and bring it up through the quilt top again at your starting point. Tug gently on the thread to pop the knot through the quilt top into the batting. This anchors the thread without an unsightly knot showing on the back. With your non-sewing hand underneath the quilt, insert the needle with the point straight down in the quilt about 1/16" from the starting point. With your underneath finger, feel for the point as the needle comes through the backing *(Figure 14)*. Place the thumb of your sewing hand approximately ½" ahead of your needle. At the moment you feel the needle touch your underneath finger, push the fabric up from below as you rock the needle down to a nearly horizontal position. Using the thumb of your sewing hand in conjunction with the underneath hand, pinch a little hill in the fabric and push the tip of the needle back through the quilt top *(Figure 15)*.

Now either push the needle all the way through to complete one stitch or rock the needle again to an upright position on its point to take another stitch. Take no more than a quarter-needleful of stitches before pulling the needle through.

When you have about 6" of thread remaining, you must end the old thread securely and invisibly. Carefully tie a knot in the thread, flat against the surface of the fabric. Pop the knot through the top as you did when beginning the line of quilting. Clip the thread, rethread your needle, and continue quilting.

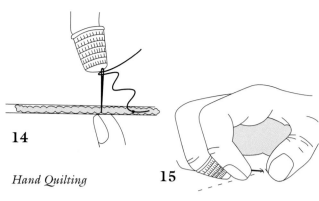

14

Hand Quilting   **15**

Machine Quilting

Machine quilting is as old as the sewing machine itself; but until recently, it was thought inferior to hand quilting. Machine quilting does, however, require a different set of skills from hand quilting.

Machine quilting can be done on your sewing machine using a straight, even stitch and a special presser foot. A walking foot, or even-feed foot, is recommended for straight-line machine quilting to help the top fabric move through the machine at the same rate that the feed dogs move the bottom fabric. With free-motion machine quilting, use a darning foot to protect your fingers and to prevent skipped stitches.

Regular sewing thread or nylon thread can be used for machine quilting. With the quilt top facing you, roll the long edges of the basted quilt toward the center of the quilt, leaving a 12"-wide area unrolled in the center. Secure the roll with bicycle clips, metal bands that are available at quilt shops. Begin at one unrolled end and fold the quilt over and over until only a small area is showing. This will be the area where you will begin to machine quilt.

Place the folded portion of the quilt in your lap. Start machine quilting in the center and work to the right side of the quilt, unfolding and unrolling the quilt as you go. Remove the quilt from the machine, turn it, and reinsert it in the machine to stitch the left side. A table placed behind your sewing machine will help support the quilt as it is stitched.

Curves and circles are most easily made by free-motion machine quilting. Using a darning foot and with the feed dogs down, move the quilt under the needle with movements of your fingertips. Place your fingertips on the fabric on each side of the presser foot and run your machine at a steady, medium speed. The length of the stitches is determined by the rate of speed at which you move the fabric through the machine. Do not rotate the quilt; rather, move it from side to side as needed. Always stop with the needle down to keep the quilt from shifting.

Making Binding

A continuous bias strip is frequently used by quilters for all kinds of quilts but is especially recommended for quilts with curved edges. Follow these steps to make a continuous bias strip:

1. To make continuous bias binding, you'll need a square of fabric. Multiply the number of inches of binding needed by the desired width of the binding (usually 2½"). Use a calculator to find the square root of that number. That's the size square needed to make your binding.

2. Cut the square in half diagonally.

3. With right sides facing, join triangles to form a sawtooth as shown in *Figure 16*.

4. Press seam open. Mark off parallel lines the desired width of the binding as shown in *Figure 17*.

5. With right sides facing, align raw edges marked Seam 2. As you align the edges, extend a Seam 2 point past its natural matching point by the distance of the width of the bias strip as shown in *Figure 18*. Join.

6. Cut the binding in a continuous strip, starting with the protruding point and following the marked lines around the tube.

7. Press the binding strip in half lengthwise, with wrong sides facing. This gives you double-fold, or French-fold, binding, which is sturdier than single-fold binding.

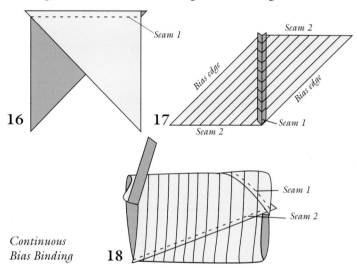

Continuous Bias Binding   **18**

Attaching Binding

To prepare your quilt for binding, baste the layers together ¼" from the edge of the quilt. Trim the backing and batting even with the edge of the quilt top. Beginning at the midpoint of one side of the quilt, pin the binding to the top, with right sides facing and raw edges aligned.

Stitch the binding along one edge of the quilt, sewing through all layers. If you are machine-stitching, backstitch at the beginning of the seam to lock the stitching.

Stitch until you reach the seam line point at the corner, and backstitch. Lift the presser foot and turn the quilt to stitch along the next edge. Continue stitching around the edge. Join the beginning and ending of the binding strip by machine, or stitch one end by hand to overlap the other.

Turn the binding to the back side and blindstitch in place. At each corner, fold the excess binding neatly and blindstitch in place.

RESOURCES

Page 61: Darlene Christopherson's appliqué patterns, including simple projects as well as the intricate quilts she is known for, are available by mail at 496 Bend of the Bosque Road, China Spring, TX 76633.

Index to Quilt Smart Techniques

Metric Conversion Chart

⅛ "	3 mm	⅛ yard	0.11 m
¼ "	6 mm	¼ yard	0.23 m
⅜ "	9 mm	⅜ yard	0.34 m
½ "	1.3 cm	½ yard	0.46 m
⅝ "	1.6 cm	⅝ yard	0.57 m
¾ "	1.9 cm	¾ yard	0.69 m
⅞ "	2.2 cm	⅞ yard	0.80 m
1 "	2.5 cm	1 yard	0.91 m

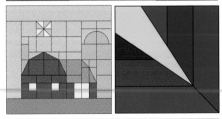